EXPLORERS AND DISCOVERY

EXPLORERS AND DISCOVERY

A REFERENCE
FIRST BOOK

BY CASS R. SANDAK
DRAWINGS BY
ANNE CANEVARI GREEN

FRANKLIN WATTS
NEW YORK/LONDON/TORONTO
SYDNEY/1983

Photographs courtesy of
the New York Public Library Picture Collection:
pp. 7, 12, 14, 16, 18, 31, 35, 39, 62, 69, and 82;
The Metropolitan Museum of Art: p. 23; n.c.: p. 25 and 26;
the Library of Congress: p. 28; the National Portrait Gallery: p. 32;
the Smithsonian Institution: p. 38; NASA: pp. 40, 79, and 80;
Culver Pictures, Inc.: pp. 45, 50, and 53;
Department of the Interior Geological Survey (DSPS/Global Marine, Inc.):
p. 86 (left); and the U.S. Navy: p.86 (right).

Library of Congress Cataloging in Publication Data

Sandak, Cass R.
Explorers and discovery.

(A Reference first book)
Summary: A dictionary detailing the achievements
of famous and lesser-known explorers, and listing
the geographical areas explored by them.
1. Explorers—Biography—Juvenile literature.
2. Discoveries (in geography)—Dictionaries, Juvenile.
[1. Explorers.   2. Discoveries (in geography)—
Dictionaries]   I. Green, Anne Canevari, ill.
II. Title.   III. Series.
G175.S324 1983   910′.922 [920]   82-17542
ISBN 0-531-04537-4

FOR JUDIE MILLS,
WHO ALWAYS MAKES
BEAUTIFUL BOOKS

EXPLORERS AND DISCOVERY

Cape
Bon

GULF OF
SIDRA

Suez
Canal

Sinai
Peninsula

MT. TOUBKAL ▲

Libyan
Desert

LAKE
NASSER

Cape
Blanc

Sahara Desert

Nubian
Desert

Cape
Verde

Senegal R.

Niger R.

S u d a n

LAKE
CHAD

MT. RAS DASHAN ▲

Cape
Guardafui

Blue Nile R.

LAKE
VOLTA

Niger R.

Benue R.

White Nile

LAKE
RUDOLF

Cape
Palmas

▲ MT.
CAMEROON

Ubangi R.

MT.
MARGHERITA ▲

LAKE
VICTORIA

▲ MT. KENYA

Cape
Lopez

Congo R.

STANLEY
FALLS

Lualaba R.

LAKE
TANGANYIKA

▲ MT.
KILIMANJARO

Namib Desert

Kasai R.

Zambezi R.

LAKE
NYASA

Cape
Delgado

Cubango R.

Zambezi R.

VICTORIA
FALLS

Kalahari
Desert

Limpopo R.

Orange R.

Vaal R.

Cape of
Good Hope

Cape Agulhas

AFRICA. Continent in the Eastern Hemisphere south of the Mediterranean Sea and joined to Asia on the northeast. Because the Mediterranean Sea was not a barrier but a highway of trade and communication, the Mediterranean coast of North Africa has been well known since ancient times. It was the site of the highly advanced civilizations of Egypt and later Carthage and other early cultures. The ancient Romans may have penetrated the interior of Africa, but most of the continent south of the Sahara Desert remained relatively unexplored by Europeans until the nineteenth century.

In 1364 French sailors from Dieppe are said to have founded colonies on the Guinea coast of Africa and in the Canary Islands, off the coast of Morocco in Northwest Africa. Over the next four centuries, other coastal settlements were established by explorers from Portugal, the Netherlands, and Britain.

In 1770 James Bruce traveled to the source of the Blue Nile. In 1778 the African Association was founded in Britain to promote exploration and later merged with the Royal Geographical Society. Richard Burton, Mungo Park, John Speke, David Livingstone, Henry Stanley, and Heinrich Barth were the principal nineteenth-century figures who, along with many others, explored and charted Africa's rivers and lakes, deserts, jungles, and mountainous regions and reported on the great natural wealth of the continent.

AGE OF DISCOVERY. The period from the fifteenth to the eighteenth centuries in Western civilization when many of the most important European explorations were undertaken. Great discoveries were made then, and many parts of the world outside of Europe and the Mediterranean were explored and mapped for the first time.

ALARCÓN, HERNANDO DE (active 1540). Spanish explorer in the American Southwest. Alarcón's voyage up the Gulf of California in the summer of 1540 proved that Lower (Baja) California was not an island but a peninsula extending from the North American landmass. Alarcón also discovered and explored the lower waters of the Colorado River.

ALDRIN, EDWIN EUGENE ("BUZZ"), JR. (b. 1930). The second man to walk on the surface of the moon. A graduate of the U.S. Military Academy and Massachusetts Institute of Technology, Aldrin became an Air Force pilot and flew combat missions in the Korean War. In 1963 he was selected as an astronaut by the National Aeronautics and Space Administration. He served as copilot of the *Eagle*, the lunar landing module on the historic *Apollo 11* mission to the moon, and walked on the moon on July 20, 1969—just a few minutes after Neil Armstrong.

ALVARADO, PEDRO DE (1485?–1541). Chief officer under Hernán Cortés in 1520, during the conquest of the Aztec civilization in the area of modern Mexico. When the Aztecs expelled the Spaniards from their capital city, Tenochtitlán, Alvarado was the last of Cortés' men to escape. Using his lance, he pole-vaulted to safety over one of the canals surrounding the city.

In 1523 Alvarado led the conquest of the native populations in the regions now known as Guatemala, El Salvador, and, later, Honduras, exploring these Central American lands as he searched for gold and Indian slaves. His achievements were recognized by the Spanish crown, and in 1530 he was appointed to a governorship in the lands he had explored.

AMAZON RIVER. South America's greatest river and the second longest river in the world—about 3,900 miles (6,240 km) long. The Amazon contains more water than any other river on earth, and its basin drains parts of Bolivia, Peru, Ecuador, Colombia, Venezuela, and Brazil.

The river was first discovered in 1500 by one of Columbus' men, the captain of the *Niña*, Vicente Yáñez Pinzón, who sailed into the river's mouth. However, the Amazon was not fully explored until Francisco de Orellana sailed down it in 1541.

AMUNDSEN, ROALD (1872–1928). Norwegian explorer. From 1903 to 1906 Amundsen navigated the Northwest Passage. He was the first person to do this. Later he became the first person to reach the South Pole.

After Robert Peary beat him in the race to be first to reach the North Pole, Amundsen turned his interest to the South Pole. A swift dog team and skis carried him to the South Pole just thirty-five days before Robert F. Scott got there. Amundsen reached his destination on December 14, 1911.

Having conquered the Antarctic, Amundsen again turned his attention to the North Pole. In 1918 he set sail from Scandinavia in order to find the Northeast Passage to the Far East. After two winters he became only the second man to sail along the entire northern coast of the Eurasian landmass. Baron Nils Adolf Erik Nordenskjöld had been the first to complete the voyage, in 1879.

**Roald Amundsen,
1872–1928**

In 1925 Amundsen began to explore the Arctic regions by aircraft. He was killed in 1928 while attempting to rescue the Italian navigator Umberto Nobile, whose plane had crashed in the polar regions.

Amundsen greatly enhanced our knowledge of Antarctica. He wrote a number of books about his explorations that have been translated into English, including *North West Passage* (1908), *The South Pole* (1912), and *My Life as an Explorer* (1927).

ANTARCTICA (or ANTARCTIC CONTINENT). Body of land surrounding the South Pole and the fifth largest continent.

Captain James Cook sailed within the Antarctic Circle and sighted the continent of Antarctica during his second Pacific voyage, from 1772 to 1775. In 1820 Fabian von Bellingshausen sailed a ship around Antarctica for the first time. James Weddell sailed through the floating ice masses that border Antarctica and discovered the sea that now bears his name, the Weddell Sea, in 1823. On an expedition from 1837 to 1840, the French explorer Dumont d'Urville explored the Adélie coast of Antarctica south of Australia. James Clark Ross led a British expedition to the South Magnetic Pole in 1839. He stayed on, exploring Antarctica for nearly five years.

In the early twentieth century, Robert Scott, Ernest Shackleton, and Douglas Mawson made epic journeys to Antarctica that greatly advanced our knowledge of the continent. Roald Amundsen of Norway was the first man to reach the South Pole, on December 14, 1911. From 1929 until his death in 1957, Admiral Richard E. Byrd led many Antarctic expeditions for the United States.

Since World War II, many nations have accelerated their scientific exploration of Antarctica. Sir Edmund Hillary and Sir Vivian Fuchs have been active in Antarctic exploration, particularly during the International Geophysical Year expedition of 1957 to 1958. Scientific stations, particularly those sponsored by the United States, continue explorations in Antarctica today, seeking information about our planet's weather and climate, plant and animal life, and mineral deposits of this, the southernmost continent.

ARCTIC REGIONS. *See* NORTH POLE.

ARMSTRONG, NEIL ALDEN (b. 1930). The first person to walk on the moon.

Armstrong was a test pilot for the National Aeronautics and Space Administration when he was chosen to become an astronaut in 1962. In 1969 he was appointed mission commander for the historic *Apollo 11* flight to the moon. On July 20, 1969, as he stepped down from the ladder of the *Eagle*, the lunar landing module, onto the surface of the moon for the first time, he said: "That's one small step for a man, one giant leap for mankind."

ASIA. Continental landmass joined to Europe in the Eastern Hemisphere. The traditional border between Asia and Europe is formed by the Ural and Caucasus mountain ranges.

European explorers were lured into Asian discoveries by the promise of Oriental luxuries—spices, silks, and precious stones. Under Alexander the Great, the ancient Greeks had pressed as far east as Afghanistan and Turkestan and into India. A Mongol king known as Genghis Khan had conquered much of Asia and had reached Europe. The peace achieved by Europeans with him and his grandson, Kublai Khan, in the thirteenth century enabled the Venetians Niccolo Polo, his brother Maffeo, and Niccolo's son Marco to journey through Asia in relative safety. Marco Polo's book on his travels was read by many and greatly influenced explorers after him. Like Marco Polo, Giovanni Carpini, a Franciscan monk, had also crossed the Asian landmass, though earlier in the thirteenth century, visiting the major cities and kingdoms.

After the collapse of the overland trade routes eastward from the Italian city-states, advances in the science of navigation led to the discovery of new routes. In 1498 the Portuguese explorer Vasco da Gama sailed to India. Russian Cossacks penetrated northern Asia and Siberia and reached the Pacific Ocean by the mid-1600s. Portuguese, French, Dutch, and English groups founded trading companies in the seventeenth century and extended European influence in Asia, but many parts of the continent—especially the mountains and deserts of central Asia—remained unknown.

In the eighteenth and nineteenth centuries, a reawakening of interest in science and exploration prompted Europeans to explore portions of Asia that were still virtually unknown, including the territories from Arabia to Siberia. Karsten Niebuhr spent several years in Arabia. John Burckhardt and Charles Doughty explored the Middle East. Sites in central Asia became the destination of a new wave of explorers, including Sven Hedin, Mark Stein, and Francis Younghusband. A Russian, Nikolai Przhevalski, explored central Asia continuously from 1867 to 1885, filling in many gaps in the world's knowledge of that area. The French explorer Francis Garnier explored Southeast Asia, and the German Baron Ferdinand von Richthofen's explorations in China led to publication, in the late nineteenth century, of the first accurate atlas of that country.

ATLANTIC OCEAN. The ocean that separates North and South America from Europe and Africa.

The Phoenicians were probably the first explorers to sail out of the Mediterranean Sea into the then-unknown Atlantic. By 1100 B.C., they had founded a trading settlement at Gades (Cadiz), Spain, north of Gibraltar. Their ships plied the waves of the North Atlantic with cargoes of tin from England and amber from the shores of the Baltic Sea. Around 325 B.C., the Greek mariner Pytheas set out from the colony at Massilia (Marseilles) in France and visited the British Isles and possibly Scandinavia. In Roman times commerce existed between the Mediterranean and the British Isles, the farthest outpost of the Roman Empire.

After A.D. 800, the Vikings began to frequent North Atlantic waters, progressing from Scandinavia to the British Isles, Iceland, and then Greenland in about 982. Viking explorers probably crossed the Atlantic to North America about A.D. 1000. Portuguese mariners explored the Atlantic coast of Africa in the fifteenth century.

After Columbus opened up the Western Hemisphere, the Atlantic coasts of North and South America were investigated by Spanish mariners and later by Portuguese, English, French, and Dutch explorers.

AUSTRALIA. Continent of the Southern Hemisphere between the Pacific and Indian oceans.

For centuries geographers and philosophers had theorized that there was a great continent in the South Pacific. They reasoned that it acted as a kind of balance for the continental landmasses of the Northern Hemisphere. Portuguese and Spanish mariners in the Pacific actually claimed to have sighted a great southern continent, but the first reliable report of Australian exploration comes from Willem Janszoon of Holland, who explored the northern coast of Australia in 1605 or 1606.

In 1699 William Dampier, an Englishman, explored the northwestern coast, its waters, and nearby islands and declared the continent unfit for habitation. In 1770 Captain James Cook explored the eastern coast and claimed it for England. In 1829 Britain claimed the entire continent and continued its already active program of colonization and settlement of the area.

In the nineteenth century a number of adventurers explored various parts of the continent for the first time. These included Robert O'Hara Burke and William John Wills, who lost their lives in the attempt, Edward John Eyre, Matthew Flinders, Friedrich Leichhardt, John McDouall Stuart, and Charles Sturt.

BAFFIN, WILLIAM (c. 1584–1622). British explorer of northeastern Canada. Baffin served as ship's pilot on two voyages that set out to discover the Northwest Passage to India and the Orient. In 1615, on the first of these voyages, he explored Hudson Bay. The following year, on his second expedition, he discovered the very northerly, ice-clogged Baffin Bay and Baffin Island. Before Sir John Ross again sighted Baffin Bay in 1818, many people had begun to doubt that it really existed.

BALBOA, VASCO NUÑEZ DE (c. 1475–1519). Spanish explorer.

The vast Pacific Ocean covers a major part of the earth's surface, but it was not until the sixteenth century that it was discovered by Europeans. In late September 1513, the Spanish conquistador Balboa became the first European to set eyes upon it.

Balboa first came to the New World in 1501 with Rodrigo de Bastidas and settled on the island of Hispaniola. In 1510 he fled to Panama to escape creditors. In Panama Balboa seized the reins of government from his rival, Martini Fernandez de Encisco, whom he had beheaded.

Balboa won the respect, support, and friendship of the native Panamanians, many of whom accompanied him on his difficult march across the narrow Isthmus of Panama. When he reached the Pacific shore he claimed the ocean and all the lands washed by it for Spain. Balboa called his discovery the Great South Sea. It was the finding of this body of water that convinced the Spaniards that they were indeed exploring a new world and not just a previously unknown portion of India.

**Vasco Nuñez de Balboa,
c. 1475–1519**

BARENTS (or BARENTZ), WILLEM (d. 1597). Dutch navigator. Barents was one of the earliest and most important of all the Arctic explorers. In three voyages he managed to investigate a vast expanse of area within the Arctic Circle while looking for the Northeast Passage to the Orient. In 1594 and again in 1595 he reached the islands of Novaya Zemlya, north of Russia, before returning home.

In 1596, on his third voyage, Barents discovered the islands of Spitsbergen, but his ship was later trapped in the ice. In the spring of 1597, after spending the winter stranded in the Arctic, Barents and his crew tried to return to the mainland in two small boats. Unfortunately, Barents did not live to complete the voyage. With the accurate navigational charts he prepared and careful meteorological information he collected, however, he made lasting contributions to our knowledge of the Arctic.

BARTH, HEINRICH (1821–1865). German scientist, linguist, and geographer who became one of the most important explorers of Africa in the nineteenth century. Barth was assigned to a British government expedition to Africa in 1850, and when the other leaders of the party died, Barth took charge. Motivated by scientific interest, he spent five years exploring central Africa south of the Sahara, including the regions around Lake Chad and the river Niger, as well as the cities of Sokoto in the Fulani Empire and Timbuktu in the Tucolor Empire.

BECKNELL, WILLIAM (1790–1832). American trader who discovered the Santa Fe Trail. This was a new and shorter route from St. Louis, Missouri, to Santa Fe, in the region that is now New Mexico. In 1822 Becknell pioneered the successful use of wagons to carry settlers and their supplies across the plains into the West—an idea that was to become very popular. The territory that Becknell's train of three wagons entered was unexplored desert. When the party ran out of water, some of Becknell's men drank the blood of their own dogs. Luckily, they soon stumbled upon the Cimarron River, where they quenched their thirsts. This led them almost directly to Santa Fe.

BEEBE, CHARLES WILLIAM (1877–1962). American naturalist, explorer, and writer. In a long career with the New York Zoological Society, as curator of its ornithology (bird) department and tropical research director, Beebe made expeditions to the West Indies, the Orient, and Central and South America. In 1934 he descended more than half a mile under the sea (about 900 m) in a bathysphere, an undersea exploration vessel similar to a small submarine. This record was not to be exceeded for many years.

Beebe was the author of numerous works on natural history, including *Galapagos* (1923), *Beneath Tropic Seas* (1928), and *Half Mile Down* (1934).

BELLINGSHAUSEN, FABIAN VON (1779–1852). An Estonian by birth, Bellingshausen made a voyage to Antarctica from 1819 to 1820 on behalf of the Russian czar. He became the first person ever to sail around the entire continent.

BERING, VITUS JONASSEN (1681–1741). Danish explorer whom the Russians hired to search for a Northeast Passage to the Far East. Commissioned by Peter the Great in 1725, Bering led an expedition into the Arctic regions of

Siberia for the purpose of mapping them. In 1728 he discovered the sea named for him and the Bering Strait, which separates Asia from Alaska. On a later expedition, after exploring Alaska, he died on the island that would be named for him.

Painting depicting the death of Vitus Bering on Bering Island in 1741

BINGER, LOUIS GUSTAVE (1856–1936). French explorer whose expeditions to West Africa, starting in 1887, greatly increased our knowledge of the ''Dark Continent.'' Binger explored the region between Bamako, Mali, and Grand Bassam, including much of the area that now makes up the countries of Ghana and the Ivory Coast. In the course of his travels, he discovered the sources of the Volta, one of the major rivers of Africa.

BOONE, DANIEL (1734–1820). Perhaps the most famous of the frontiersmen of the North American wilderness, and an expert trapper, woodsman, and guide. From 1769 to 1771 Boone explored the virgin forests of the Kentucky region thoroughly. This same area later became a county of Virginia.

BOUGAINVILLE, LOUIS ANTOINE DE (1729–1811). French navigator and explorer who sailed around the world on a voyage from 1767 to 1769. In the Southwest Pacific he rediscovered the Solomon Islands that had first been found by the Spanish and named the largest of them Bougainville, after himself.

BRENDAN, SAINT (d. A.D. 577?). Irish abbot who became the subject for a popular legend of the Middle Ages. The story tells how Brendan and some of his monks sailed westward and visited islands that some think may have been along the coast of North America.

BRIDGER, JAMES (1804–1881). Fur trader who became one of the most famous explorers of the American Northwest. Bridger was a mountainman who had an almost instinctive talent as a guide. For nearly fifty years he explored and led others through parts of the country where few people had ever been.

Bridger first became acquainted with the wilderness as a trapper in 1822. He was only eighteen years old at the time. By 1824 he had explored Utah thoroughly enough to discover the Great Salt Lake while trying to win a wager.

Bridger was also the first white man to explore the parts of Wyoming, Montana, and Idaho that we now know as Yellowstone Park. John Colter in 1807 had been the first to notice the geysers that dotted the area, but Bridger investigated the region more completely.

In 1830 Bridger led the first wagon train across the Oregon Trail into the Northwest. In 1843 he founded Fort Bridger, a supply post set up to aid travelers along the trail. And in the years that followed he helped thousands of settlers who came to the West, serving as protector and guide.

BURKE, ROBERT O'HARA (1820–1861). Irish-born explorer who immigrated to Australia in 1853. In 1860, Burke and William John Wills, an astronomer from Melbourne, led an expedition of about a dozen men across the Australian continent from south to north. Leaving from Menindee in the southeast, they traveled to the Gulf of Carpentaria on Australia's northern coast. However, on the return journey, both Wills and Burke succumbed to starvation and exposure. Rescue parties seeking traces of the ill-fated expedition added greatly to our knowledge of central Australia.

BURTON, SIR RICHARD FRANCIS (1821–1890). English writer and adventurer who traveled through the Islamic world in various Arab disguises. In 1853 Burton became one of the first non-Muslims to visit the shrines at Mecca and Medina. In 1864 he traveled to Harar in Ethiopia. And in 1858 he discovered Lake Tanganyika. Later Burton wrote lively accounts of his travels, which had included extensive explorations in Africa and Brazil.

BYRD, RICHARD EVELYN (1888–1957). American polar explorer who took up the new science of aviation in 1917. In 1926 Byrd and Floyd Bennett flew across the North Pole, and in 1927 he and three companions made a transatlantic flight. In 1929 Byrd led an expedition to Antarctica, where he discovered and named the Rockefeller Range and Marie Byrd Land. Later that year he and a companion flew to the South Pole and back.

Byrd led four more expeditions to Antarctica—in 1933, from 1939 to 1940, from 1946 to 1947, and from 1955 to 1956. In 1955 the U.S. Navy made Admiral Byrd commander of all American operations in Antarctica. Byrd's expeditions are the basis for U.S. claims to territory there.

**Admiral
Richard E. Byrd,
1888–1957**

CABEZA DE VACA, ALVAR NUÑEZ (1490?–?1557). Spanish adventurer and the first European to cross North America. In 1528 Lieutenant Cabeza de Vaca and his crew, acting on orders from their commander, reached Tampa, Florida, and set out on foot looking for suitable land for settlement. Reaching the Florida Panhandle, they fled from hostile Indians and tried to sail on crude barges across the Gulf of Mexico. But Cabeza de Vaca and a few others foundered on the beach near modern-day Galveston, Texas, where they were captured by Indians and held prisoner for five years.

Cabeza de Vaca was appalled by the habits of his captors, who subsisted on a diet of spiders, insects, and animal dung. In 1536 he and three others managed to escape and cross Texas to the Spanish settlement of Ures, near Mexico's Pacific coast. His adventures had taken him across the entire breadth of North America, from Florida to the Pacific coast.

CABOT, JOHN (flourished 1461–1498). Explorer of the New World for England.

John Cabot was Italian by birth and shared Columbus' enthusiasm for reaching the Far East by sailing west. However, there is no reason to believe that either explorer was aware of or was influenced by the other.

In the 1480s Cabot went to England and lived for a while in the seaport of Bristol. In 1497 he was sent by Henry VII to search for a northerly route to China. He sailed from Bristol and reached the North American coast at Newfoundland or Cape Breton Island. He thought he had reached Asia. His explorations were the basis for English claims to North American lands.

In 1498 Cabot again sailed for North America, but little is known of this expedition. No records exist to indicate whether or not it proved successful or even whether any of the crew ever returned.

The departure of John and Sebastian Cabot from Bristol on their first voyage of discovery. Painting by Ernest Loard.

CABOT, SEBASTIAN (1483–1557). Son of the great English explorer John Cabot. Sebastian may have gone along on his father's famous voyage of 1497.

In 1509 Sebastian Cabot made a voyage for England in search of the Northwest Passage to the Far East. Scholars believe that he may have reached Hudson Bay.

In 1512 Cabot went to Spain to serve in the Spanish Navy. By 1518 he had risen to the position of chief pilot. In 1526 he was put in charge of an expedition to the Moluccas, Indonesian islands near Malaysia, to bring back spices. Instead, he led his ship into Rio de la Plata country and spent several years exploring the Paraguay, Plata, and Parana rivers in South America. He might never have left, but lack of food and hostile Indian tribes forced him to return to Spain in 1530. There he found only discredit and dishonor.

In 1548 Cabot reentered service to England. By 1553 he had become governor of a company organized to promote the search for a Northeast Passage to the Orient. Cabot did not make any more of his own voyages, but he persuaded Sir Hugh Willoughby to lead an expedition in an attempt to open up trade with China.

CABRAL, PEDRO ALVARES (c. 1467–1520). Portuguese navigator who was sent by the king of Portugal in 1500 to round the coast of Africa on his way to India. His ship was reputedly blown off course, far to the west, and instead of Africa he reached the coast of Brazil, which he then claimed for Portugal. Bartolomeu Dias accompanied Cabral on this voyage, as one of his officers. Cabral left Brazil and sailed southeast, then around the Cape of Good Hope and across the Indian Ocean, finally arriving in the Indian city of Calicut.

CAILLÉ, RENÉ AUGUSTE (1799–1838). French explorer. Caillé was the first European to reach the city of Timbuktu near the Niger River and to return home again. He undertook the journey partly to win a cash prize of 1,000 francs from the Paris Geographical Society. He taught himself Arabic and disguised himself as a Muslim for the journey. After recovering from a serious illness, he arrived in 1828 at Timbuktu, where he stayed briefly before returning to France to collect his prize money.

CAMERON, VERNEY LOVETT (1844-1894). English Navy officer sent to Africa by the Royal Geographical Society in 1873 to aid explorer and missionary David Livingstone. When he arrived in Zanzibar and found that Livingstone was already dead, Cameron stayed on anyway, exploring for two years the area drained by the Congo River. He became the first European to cross Equatorial Africa from sea to sea, beginning in Zanzibar and ending up in Benguela on the Angola coast.

CANADA. Country in northern North America.

The Vikings were probably the first Europeans to travel to North America and set up settlements along the coast of Canada. These settlements died out, however, and it was not until the arrival of John Cabot in 1497 that Canada was explored again by Europeans. Cabot was seeking a Northwest Passage to China for the English king, Henry VII. He explored the area around Nova Scotia or Newfoundland and returned to England with tales of rich fishing waters. But the English did not assert their claims to Canada until later.

In 1534 Jacques Cartier claimed the Gaspé Peninsula for France. Samuel de Champlain first visited the area called New France in 1603. In 1608 he returned with settlers to found the city of Quebec. France called this portion of the New

World "Acadia" (today's eastern Canada), and their claim extended west as far as Lake Superior and down the Mississippi River to its mouth, where French settlers founded New Orleans. French explorers of this early period included Jean Nicolet, Père Marquette, Louis Joliet, and Robert La Salle.

In 1763, Britain wrested control of Canada from the French in the Seven Years' War, and British explorers such as Sir Alexander Mackenzie extended our knowledge of the western Canadian frontier. Canada remains a part of the British Commonwealth to this day.

CANO, JUAN SEBASTIÁN DEL (c. 1476–1526). The Spanish navigator who commanded the ship *Concepción* under Magellan, during Magellan's historic expedition around the world. After Magellan's death in the Philippines, del Cano took command of the remaining ships and men and arrived in Spain with the *Victoria* and eighteen sailors on September 6, 1522. He was thus the first person to circumnavigate the globe. In 1525 del Cano set out on a second voyage following Magellan's route, but he died while crossing the Pacific Ocean.

CAPE HORN. The piece of land jutting out from the southernmost tip of South America. It was discovered by the Dutch navigator Willem Schouten, who first rounded it on January 29, 1616. Schouten named the passage after the Dutch town of Hoorn, his birthplace in the Netherlands. Strong currents and frequent storms made "rounding the Horn" one of the most difficult passages in the days of sailing ships.

CAPE OF GOOD HOPE. The southern tip of Africa, first rounded by the Portuguese navigator Bartolomeu Dias in 1488. Dias named it the Cape of Storms, but King John II later changed the name to the Cape of Good Hope.

CÁRDENAS, GARCIA LÓPEZ DE (active 1540). Spanish explorer in the American Southwest. Cárdenas was a member of Francisco Coronado's fruitless expedition in search of the Seven Cities of Cibola. After Coronado heard Hopi Indian reports of a great river to the west, Cárdenas was selected to lead a party to search for the river. Twenty days' march through New Mexico brought him and his men to the Grand Canyon, formed by the Colorado River. He and his men thus became the first Europeans to see the canyon. The river itself, however, had been discovered a month earlier, by Hernando de Alarcón.

CARPINI, GIOVANNI DE PIANO (c. 1180–1252). Early traveler to the Far East. In 1245 Pope Innocent IV dispatched Carpini, a Franciscan monk, as an emissary to the Mongols in Asia. Carpini started from Lyons, France, and followed an overland route through Kiev, Russia, passing north of the Caspian Sea across central Asia to the court of the Great Khan at Karakorum in Mongolia. Carpini and the Polish Friar Benedict covered the 3,000 miles (4,800 km) on horseback in only 106 days. Carpini returned to Europe in 1247 with a lively account of his travels that aroused the interest of others, including the Venetian merchants Niccolo and Maffeo Polo, father and uncle, respectively, of Marco Polo.

CARTERET, PHILIP (d. 1796). British rear admiral and captain of the sloop *Swallow*, which accompanied Samuel Wallis on his crossing of the South Pacific in 1766. The *Swallow* was accidentally separated from Wallis' ship near Tierra del Fuego, just off the coast of South America. Carteret continued across the Pacific alone and in 1767 discovered several previously unknown islands, including Pitcairn Island, southeast of the Tuamotu Archipelago. The island was first sighted by Robert Pitcairn, a midshipman on the *Swallow*. Carteret also rediscovered the Solomon and Santa Cruz islands first found by Mendaña de Neyra on a voyage from 1567 to 1568.

CARTIER, JACQUES (1491–1557). French navigator. Cartier was the discoverer of the St. Lawrence River and the first European to explore the Gulf of St. Lawrence. He made three voyages to the New World for Francis I to find a passage to the Far East. On his first voyage, in 1534, he landed on the coast of the Gaspé Peninsula, in what is now the province of Quebec, and claimed the area for France.

On his second voyage, from 1535 to 1536, Cartier sailed up the St. Lawrence River to the site of the modern city of Quebec and visited the Indian settlement of Hochelaga, where Montreal now stands. On Cartier's third voyage, from 1541 to 1542, he returned to the coast near Newfoundland and devoted himself to trying, unsuccessfully, to colonize parts of Canada. Cartier failed in his attempt to locate a Northwest Passage, but his discoveries were the basis for French claims to the St. Lawrence valley and, later, to other portions of North America.

CHAMPLAIN, SAMUEL DE (1567–1635). French explorer who was the principal founder of New France (Canada). Champlain's first three-year voyage to the New World (1586–1589) took him to the West Indies, Mexico, and Panama. In 1603 he joined a fur-trading expedition to New France and traveled up the St. Lawrence River as far as the Lachine Rapids before returning to France.

In 1604 Champlain set out again with Sieur de Monts, a French nobleman, to found a colony at the mouth of the St. Croix River, between modern-day Maine and Canada. The colony was moved in 1605 to Port Royal in Acadia (eastern Canada) and was attacked by British settlers from the colony of Jamestown, thereby beginning the British-French rivalry for North America.

Over the next four years, Champlain explored along the eastern coast of Canada and New England. He discovered most of Maine's principal rivers and made the first accurate maps of the New England coast as far south as Martha's Vineyard. After only a few years, the Port Royal colony failed, but in 1608 Champlain brought a new shipload of colonists to settle the community of Quebec at a site on the St. Lawrence River. The following spring, he traveled south with a war party of Huron Indians and discovered the long body of water between New York and Vermont that now bears his name—Lake Champlain.

In 1612 Champlain returned to France to obtain a new fur-trading charter. In 1613 he was back in New France to begin a journey to the Great Lakes region. By 1615 he had explored Lake Huron and Lake Ontario. After 1616 Champlain did no more exploring but devoted himself to making the Quebec colony a success. In 1629 Quebec was seized by the British, and Champlain spent four years in England as an exile.

In 1632 New France became a French colony once again, and Champlain returned to it. He encouraged his friend, Jean Nicolet, to continue exploring, and in 1634 Nicolet extended French territorial claims as far west as modern-day Wisconsin.

CLAPPERTON, HUGH (1788–1827). British explorer in West Africa. Clapperton, in 1823, became one of the discoverers of Lake Chad.

It was Clapperton's dream to locate the mouth of the great Niger River. No one knew whether the river flowed into the sea, into an unknown lake, into the river Nile, or into an underground cavern. Clapperton died before he could prove his theory that the Niger empties into the Gulf of Guinea. However, his servant, Richard Lander, continued Clapperton's work and eventually succeeded in tracing the course of the Niger.

CLARK, WILLIAM (1770–1838). American explorer and one of the leaders of the Lewis and Clark expedition. In 1803 Meriwether Lewis, secretary to President Thomas Jefferson, asked Clark to accompany him on an overland expedition to the Pacific that Lewis was then organizing at the encouragement of Jefferson, who wanted the Missouri and Columbia rivers explored. Clark's sensitive observations of nature added to the fund of knowledge gained by this famous expedition, and his journals and maps provided an invaluable record of the journey. *See also* LEWIS AND CLARK EXPEDITION.

COLLINS, MICHAEL (b. 1930). American astronaut. Collins graduated from the U.S. Military Academy and became an Air Force test pilot. He was selected as an astronaut for the U.S. space agency, NASA, in 1963. In July 1969 he served as pilot of the command module *Columbia* on the historic *Apollo 11* mission to the moon. He stayed aboard the *Columbia* while Neil Armstrong and Buzz Aldrin descended to the moon's surface using the lunar lander, the *Eagle*.

Christopher Columbus, 1451?–1506

COLUMBUS, CHRISTOPHER (1451?–1506). Discoverer of the New World.
Christopher Columbus was born and raised in the Italian port city of Genoa. He went to sea at an early age and, prior to his crossing of the Atlantic, made several lengthy voyages to various ports on the Mediterranean, to Ireland and Iceland, and to the Guinea coast of Africa. He settled in Portugal after finding himself shipwrecked there, became a chart and map maker, and married a Portuguese woman.

Because he subscribed to the theory that the earth was round and not flat, and possibly because of his reading of the Norse sagas and the writings of Marco Polo and others, Columbus became convinced that he could reach the Orient by sailing west across the Atlantic. He spent seven years trying to get financial support for his venture. He appealed to the senate of his native city of Genoa, to the kings of Portugal and England, and to other wealthy people.

Finally, on April 17, 1492, Ferdinand and Isabella, the king and queen of Spain, agreed to pay for the trip. They were eager to find a route to the Orient that was not already used by the Portuguese. A little more than three months later, on August 3, 1492, Columbus, a crew of about 120 men, and three small ships set sail from the Spanish port of Palos. Columbus himself commanded the *Santa Maria*. The *Niña* was commanded by Vicente Pinzón, and the *Pinta* was commanded by Martín Alonso Pinzón. They stopped first in the Canary Islands. After a total of ten weeks at sea, land—now believed to have been modern-day Watlings Island in the Bahamas—was sighted on October 12. Columbus named this land San Salvador. Cuba was discovered on October 28 (Columbus thought it was Japan), and the island of Hispaniola—now the site of

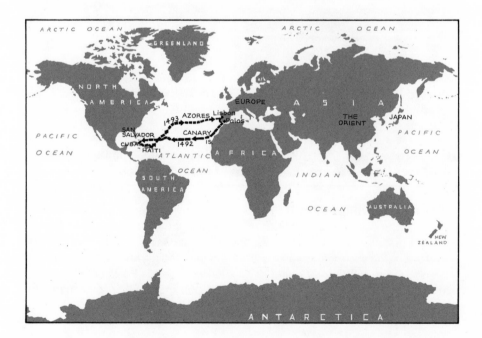

**A full-sized replica
of the *Santa Maria*,
Columbus' flagship**

Haiti and the Dominican Republic—was reached one month later. The *Santa Maria* was shipwrecked, but Columbus arrived back in Spain with the *Niña* and *Pinta* on March 15, 1493—and claimed he had been to Asia!

Columbus' discoveries brought him fame and moderate wealth. He made three additional voyages of discovery to the New World, reaching the islands of Puerto Rico, Dominica, Jamaica, and Trinidad, as well as the coast of South America. During his last voyage, from 1502 to 1504, he explored portions of Central America and part of the Gulf of Mexico. However, Columbus never realized that he had found a new world. He died believing that he had merely discovered an unknown portion of the Orient.

Today it is clear that Columbus was not the first European to cross the Atlantic and reach the Western Hemisphere. The Vikings and perhaps other mariners had preceded him. But in a very real sense, Columbus can be called the discoverer of the Americas, since his voyages were widely publicized and opened up the New World to further exploration, colonization, and development.

CONQUISTADOR. Spanish for "one who conquers." Specifically, the word is used to refer to the leaders in the Spanish conquest of the Americas in the sixteenth century, especially of Mexico and Peru.

COOK, JAMES (1728–1779). Principal English explorer of the eighteenth century.

Cook joined the Royal Navy at the age of twenty-seven, after serving an apprenticeship in a shipping firm in Whitby, England. On early voyages to England's holdings in the New World, he surveyed the St. Lawrence Channel in 1760 and from 1763 to 1767 explored the coasts of Newfoundland and Labrador.

On a scientific expedition lasting from 1768 to 1771, undertaken to chart the path of the planet Venus, Cook also explored the coasts of New Zealand and eastern Australia. He returned to England in 1771, having circumnavigated the globe.

Captain Cook lands at Botany Bay, Australia, in 1770. Painting by E. Phillips Fox.

From 1772 to 1775 Cook commanded the *Resolution* and the *Adventure* on a voyage in the South Pacific. During this journey he explored the Antarctic Ocean and the New Hebrides Islands and discovered New Caledonia. He also put to rest forever the rumor that there was a great undiscovered continent in the South Pacific.

In 1778 Cook discovered the Hawaiian Islands, which he named the Sandwich Islands, after the Earl of Sandwich. After searching unsuccessfully along North America's northwest coast for a route to the Atlantic Ocean, he returned to Hawaii, where he was killed by natives during one of their uprisings.

Cook himself kept a detailed record of his observations, in journals he kept on his voyages. He also employed artists to make visual representations of his trips. By enforcing strict dietary and sanitary codes, he kept his crew healthy and prevented their developing scurvy, a vitamin C deficiency disease that was a constant threat on lengthy voyages, when fresh fruits and vegetables were not available.

CORONADO, FRANCISCO VASQUEZ DE (c. 1510–1554). Spanish conquistador.

Coronado became governor of the Mexican province of Nueva Galicia in 1538. Two years later he was appointed captain general of a land and sea expedition to search for the fabulous riches of the Seven Cities of Cibola.

Since the cities did not exist, it is not surprising that the expeditionary force never found them. Still, members of Coronado's party did make some startling geographic discoveries. Garcia López de Cárdenas found the Grand Canyon. Pedro de Tovar traveled among the Hopi Indian villages of northern Arizona, and Hernando de Alvarado explored the Rio Grande and the Pecos River of present-day Texas.

Following other rumors of fabulously wealthy Indian kingdoms, Coronado and Alvarado traveled farther and explored portions of what is now the Texas Panhandle, Oklahoma, and Kansas. Coronado and those of his party who had remained with him returned to Mexico in 1542.

Coronado's explorations opened up new frontiers in the Southwest and brought the Spaniards into contact with the Pueblo Indians for the first time. After retiring from government life in 1544, Coronado made other forays into southern Arizona and Baja California. His extensive journeys greatly enriched our geographical knowledge of these regions. *See also* SEVEN CITIES OF CIBOLA.

CORTÉS, HERNÁN (or HERNANDO CORTEZ) (1485–1547). The Spanish conquistador who gained control of Mexico by defeating the Aztecs.

Cortés first came to the New World in 1504 on a mission to Hispaniola. In 1511 he went to Cuba and in 1518 sailed from there in command of an expedition to Mexico. He arrived at Yucatan and explored the coast with his men before deciding to march inland to the Aztec capital of Tenochtitlán, the site of present-day Mexico City. The Aztec emperor Montezuma, believing the Spaniards to be descendants of one of their gods, received Cortés warmly. Thus the Spanish had a relatively easy time taking the emperor hostage. They soon gained control of the entire empire, aided by Indian tribes who were hostile to their Aztec overlords. By 1521 the conquest was complete, and Cortés extended Spanish control throughout Mexico and into Central America.

**Hernán Cortés,
1485–1547**

COUSTEAU, JACQUES-YVES (b. 1910). French oceanographic explorer. Cousteau was an officer in the French Navy when, in 1943, along with scientist and inventor Emil Gagnon, he developed the aqualung, or self-contained underwater breathing apparatus, now called scuba. Later Cousteau helped to design the bathyscaphe, a small submarine for conducting underwater scientific research.

In 1945 Cousteau persuaded the French Navy to form a team to conduct underwater research. In 1957 Prince Rainier appointed him director of the Oceanographic Museum of Monaco.

Since 1951 Cousteau has made yearly voyages on his vessel, the *Calypso*, to conduct oceanographic research. On these trips he has been accompanied by a staff of scientists and researchers. His marine explorations have been the subject of numerous books he has written and many documentary films he has made over the years.

COVILHÃ, PEDRO DE (1440?–?1526). Adventurer hired by King John II of Portugal to explore various parts of the Middle East as well as Asia and Africa. Covilhã disguised himself as an Arab and acted as a secret agent in uncovering information about the rich ports of the East. His travels took him from Aden in Yemen to Calicut in India. From there he investigated the city of Goa, where a Portuguese colony was later established. He also spent time in Hormuz, Iran; and Sofala, Mozambique. He sent reports to the Portuguese monarch on the riches of the seaports he visited and on the navigational problems presented by the monsoon winds that blow across the Indian Ocean, but he himself never returned to Portugal. Covilhã's efforts helped Portugal to extend its empire and to become a major sea power in the fifteenth and sixteenth centuries.

DAMPIER, WILLIAM (1652?–1715). English adventurer who fought against the Dutch in 1673, then managed a Jamaican plantation for several years. From 1679 to 1681 Dampier served as a buccaneer, preying on Spanish ships off the western coast of South America.

In 1699 Dampier headed an expedition to the South Pacific and discovered the Dampier Archipelago and Dampier Strait off the west coast of Australia. On a privateering expedition from 1708 to 1711, he rescued Alexander Selkirk, a Scottish sea captain who had been marooned for several years on an island off the coast of Chile. Daniel Defoe based his famous novel, *Robinson Crusoe*, on Selkirk's story.

DARK CONTINENT. Name given to Africa by early Europeans because they knew so little about the continent. It was considered a place of mystery, inhabited by exotic people and dangerous wild animals. Many parts of Africa were not explored by Europeans until the late nineteenth century, and some remote parts of the continent remain virtually uncharted and unknown even today.

DAVYS (or DAVIS), JOHN (c. 1550–1605). English explorer whose early explorations gave map makers a clearer picture of the geography of the Arctic regions north of Labrador. Davys was looking for a passage to the Far East when he discovered the Falkland Islands in the South Atlantic in 1592. These islands are called the Malvinas by the Spanish and the Argentinians, who also claimed them. In addition to being a skilled navigator, Davys was also a successful inventor. He designed a type of quadrant, an instrument that was used for many years by sailors to determine their location at sea.

**Hernando De Soto,
1500?–1542**

DE SOTO, HERNANDO (1500?–1542). Spanish explorer.

De Soto was still in Spain when he heard about Alvar Nuñez Cabeza de Vaca's harrowing experiences in crossing North America. Convinced that the continent held more promise than Cabeza de Vaca's accounts had indicated, De Soto sailed from Spain in 1538 with a fleet of ten ships and about 620 soldiers on an expedition to conquer Florida for Spain and bring back treasure.

De Soto's party landed in Florida in 1539. Following elusive reports of gold, silver, and jewels, they marched north into the area of modern Georgia, northeast to the Savannah River, and then southwest. Periodically beset by marauding Indians, they followed the Gulf Coast through the areas that are now Alabama and Louisiana. In 1541 they became the first Europeans to see the Mississippi River. They crossed it and turned northwest into the modern regions of Arkansas and Oklahoma. After a desperate winter, De Soto decided to return to the Mississippi. In the spring of 1542, he died, and his body was buried in the Mississippi River. Roughly three hundred of his men survived to reach the Spanish settlement at Tampico, Mexico, in the autumn of 1542.

DIAS (or DIAZ), BARTOLOMEU (d. 1500). Portuguese navigator. In 1488, under the patronage of King John II of Portugal, Dias became the first European to sail around the southern tip of Africa. He called it the *Cabo Tormentoso*, or Cape of Storms, but it was later renamed the Cape of Good Hope. His voyage opened up navigation to India. Nine years later, Vasco da Gama succeeded in sailing to India following Dias' route but continuing farther north. Before this time only long and costly overland routes had been used to reach India.

In 1500 Dias accompanied Pedro Alvares Cabral on a voyage that resulted in the discovery of Brazil. Later that year, Dias died at sea during a storm off the African coast, near the Cape of Good Hope.

**Sir Francis Drake,
1540?–1596**

DRAKE, SIR FRANCIS (1540?–1596). English navigator, explorer, and the first Englishman to circumnavigate the globe.

In 1577 Drake set out with a fleet of five ships, intent on plundering Spanish settlements on the western coast of South America. Two of the ships were abandoned at the mouth of the Rio de la Plata. With the remaining three ships Drake continued south and sailed through the Strait of Magellan. One of the ships sank in a storm, and another became lost but managed to sail back to England. Drake's vessel, the *Golden Hind*, sailed up the western coast of South America, raiding Spanish settlements along the way as Drake searched, unsuccessfully, for a passage back to the Atlantic.

Drake sailed as far north as the modern state of Washington before returning to San Francisco Bay to prepare his ships to cross the Pacific. He claimed
the region of central California for Queen Elizabeth and named the area New
Albion. Then he crossed the Pacific, stopping in the Moluccas, the Celebes,
and Java. His ship crossed the Indian Ocean, sailed around Africa, and arrived
back in England in 1580 laden with treasure.

Drake was knighted by Queen Elizabeth I on board his ship. He continued to
assert English naval power, attacking Spanish ships and Spanish settlements
in the New World. And he was one of the commanders of the British fleet that
defeated the so-called "invincible" Spanish Armada in 1588.

DUMONT, D'URVILLE, JULES-SEBASTIEN-CESAR (1790–1842). French
explorer and naturalist who devoted his career to accurately mapping the
southwest Pacific. In two major expeditions, between 1826 and 1829 and from
1837 to 1840, Dumont d'Urville charted several million square miles of waters
dotted with tiny islets and containing dangerous submerged rocks. On the
second of these voyages he visited Antarctica and claimed the Adélie coast
for France, naming it after his wife.

E

EL DORADO. Name given to an imaginary country (or city) sought by many Spanish explorers and adventurers in South America. *El Dorado* means, literally, "the gilded one." It was taken from the title of the legendary South American Indian king who was thought to rule this fabulously wealthy land and was said to cover his body with gold dust at yearly festivals.

Indian legends about *El Dorado*—plus the Spaniards' greed for gold—gave rise to these stories. Though no such city or country was ever found, the search for it prompted exploration of many areas of North and South America.

ERICSSON, LEIF (fl. c. A.D. 1000). Son of the Norse chieftain Eric the Red. Leif was probably born in Iceland but journeyed with his father to the Norse settlement in Greenland. There he became a Christian and established Christianity on the island. Around the year A.D. 1002 he purchased a Viking ship owned by Bjarni Herjolfsson and sailed west from Greenland and discovered North America (probably somewhere in the area between New England and Newfoundland). Leif named the place where he landed Vinland. Old Norse sagas tell of his travels. Leif made his epic journey almost five hundred years before Columbus set sail for the New World. *See also* VIKINGS and VINLAND.

**Leif Ericsson
off the coast
of Vinland**

ERIC THE RED. (fl. late 10th century A.D.). Norse chieftain who discovered and colonized Greenland. Around A.D. 950 Eric's father, who had been exiled for manslaughter, and Eric left Norway to live in the Viking settlement in Iceland. When Eric was banished from Iceland in 982 for three years for feuding, he decided to sail in search of legendary lands west of Iceland and thus discovered Greenland. He spent the next three years exploring the south and west coasts of the vast island, then returned to Iceland in 986 to promote the Viking colonization of the new land he had discovered. He called the place Greenland to attract would-be settlers. About 986 he led a fleet of twenty-five ships and about 500 people to Greenland to found a Norse colony there. Only fourteen ships and 350 colonists survived the trip. Eric the Red's adventures are related in the Norse sagas.

FLINDERS, MATTHEW (1774–1814). Captain in the English Navy who on two lengthy expeditions (from 1795 to 1799 and 1801 to 1803) surveyed and charted the coasts of Australia and Tasmania.

FOUNTAIN OF YOUTH. Name given to a legendary spring said to be located on the island of Bimini, north of Cuba in the West Indies. The fountain's waters were supposed to be able to restore youth, health, and beauty to anyone who drank from or bathed in them. The Spanish explorer Juan Ponce de Leon discovered Florida while searching for the imaginary fountain.

FRANKLIN, SIR JOHN (1786–1847). British explorer who, from 1819 to 1822, 1825 to 1827, and 1845 to 1848 led expeditions into the Arctic regions of northern Canada. Franklin is sometimes credited with finding the Northwest Passage to the Orient during the 1845–48 expedition, since he came within a few miles of it. However, his expedition failed to return. More than forty rescue missions were sent in later years to find him and his group. These various search teams discovered an enormous amount of information about the geography of northern Canada before finding the frozen remains of Franklin's lost expedition in the 1850s.

FREMONT, JOHN CHARLES (1813–1890). American explorer known as "The Pathfinder."

Fremont began his career teaching mathematics at the U.S. Naval Academy. From 1838 to 1839 he helped to survey the area between the upper Mississippi and Missouri rivers. In 1841 the War Department appointed him to command an expedition to explore the Des Moines River. The following year he headed a Rocky Mountain expedition along with Kit Carson.

From 1843 to 1844 Fremont pressed on to Oregon and explored what is today Nevada, crossing the Sierra Nevada into California before returning home. He later returned to California and settled there. When the Mexican War broke out, Fremont encouraged the American settlers in California to revolt against the Mexican authorities, who were still in control. After the war Fremont became active in California politics and later ran unsuccessfully for president.

FROBISHER, SIR MARTIN (1535?–1594). English explorer.

As a young boy Frobisher went to sea and spent his early years with England's mercantile fleet. Sir Humphrey Gilbert inspired his interest in finding the Northwest Passage to China.

Frobisher made voyages in 1576, 1577, and 1578 to the Arctic regions to search for a sea route to the Pacific. Queen Elizabeth I and a group of merchants called the Cathay Company supported these ventures. On his first voyage he sailed into a bay later named Frobisher Bay after him and landed at South Baffin Island. He brought back from this trip samples of a black rock, believing that it contained gold. He also brought back an Eskimo, whose Asiatic features had convinced him he had reached China. The Eskimo, he thought, was proof that he had been to the Orient. On two subsequent voyages, he explored Frobisher Bay and part of the Hudson Strait. But none of his explorations brought him much fame or credit.

In 1585 Frobisher commanded a ship in Sir Francis Drake's West Indies expedition. Queen Elizabeth knighted him in 1588 for helping to defeat the Spanish Armada.

FUCHS, SIR VIVIAN ERNEST (b. 1908). British geologist and explorer. During the International Geophysical Year expedition of 1957 and 1958, Fuchs and Sir Edmund Hillary led the first overland crossing of Antarctica by way of the South Pole.

GAGARIN, YURI ALEKSEYEVICH (1934–1968). Soviet cosmonaut and the first person to travel into space. On April 12, 1961, Gagarin spent one hour and twenty-nine minutes orbiting the earth in the spacecraft *Vostok 1*. He lost his life during a test flight in 1968.

Yuri Alekseyevich Gagarin, 1934–1968

**Vasco da Gama,
c. 1469–1524**

GAMA, VASCO DA (c. 1469–1524). Portuguese navigator who became the first European to sail to India via the Cape of Good Hope. Manuel I of Portugal commissioned the sea journey, which took more than two years to complete. Following Bartolomeu Dias' success in rounding the Cape of Good Hope and sailing part of the way up Africa's eastern coast, da Gama sailed from Portugal in 1497 with a fleet of four ships. He rounded the Cape of Good Hope at Africa's southern tip and continued up the continent's eastern coast, landing at Malindi, Kenya, in 1498. After erecting a monument to his achievement, da Gama sailed east across the Indian Ocean to the city of Calicut. He returned to Portugal in 1499.

Da Gama had given instructions to Pedro Cabral on how to sail to India before Cabral began the voyage in which he accidentally discovered Brazil. In 1502 da Gama himself led a fleet of twenty ships on his second voyage to India and established Portuguese trading centers in India and along Africa's east coast. Portuguese merchants became rich in the trade for spices and other luxuries as they sought to establish a monopoly on navigation in the Indian Ocean.

GLENN, JOHN HERSCHEL, JR. (b. 1921). American astronaut. On February 20, 1962, Glenn became the first American and the third person in history to orbit the earth. Yuri Gagarin, a Russian, had been the first.

Glenn's spacecraft, the *Friendship 7*, was launched from Cape Canaveral, Florida, by an Atlas–D rocket. Glenn circled the earth three times in a flight lasting four hours and fifty-five minutes. He was retrieved from his Gemini capsule in the Atlantic Ocean near the Bahamas.

During the flight, Glenn's spacecraft achieved a maximum altitude of 187.75 miles (300.4 km) and traveled at a speed of approximately 17,500 miles (28,000 km) per hour. The entire flight covered a total distance of some 81,000 miles (129,600 km). Glenn made observations, conducted experiments, and took photographs during the trip. Today he is a U.S. senator.

John H. Glenn, Jr., in his space suit, standing beside the *Friendship 7* capsule

GRANDIDIER, ALFRED (1836–1921). French adventurer and scholar. Grandidier originally planned to explore Tibet, but in 1865 he arrived in Madagascar and spent the next five years investigating the huge African island that up to that time was largely unknown. He made an exhaustive survey of Madagascar and visited all its major towns, collecting hundreds of specimens of plants, animals, and minerals in addition to information about the people who lived there.

GRAY, ROBERT (1755–1806). American ship's captain who discovered the Columbia River (named after his ship, the *Columbia*) that rises in British Columbia and empties into the Pacific near Astoria, Oregon, cutting through the Cascade and coastal mountain ranges of the northwestern United States. Gray was also the first American to sail around the globe, on a voyage lasting from 1787 to 1790.

GREENLAND. Large island in the North Atlantic between Canada and Iceland. Much of Greenland is within the Arctic Circle. The Norse chieftain Eric the Red discovered and colonized it around A.D. 982, although there had been prior Eskimo settlements there for an unknown length of time.

HAKLUYT, RICHARD (1552?–1616). English writer and geographer of the Elizabethan period. Hakluyt wrote a number of well-known books on British explorations throughout the world and published accounts of the travels of other explorers, including Hernando de Soto, Sir Humphrey Gilbert, and Sir Walter Raleigh. Both as a lecturer in geography at Oxford University and as a member of the Virginia Company of London, Hakluyt encouraged the British settlement of North America.

HANNO (d. 480 B.C.). Phoenician navigator from Carthage. Hanno drew upon the knowledge of centuries of Phoenician seafarers and was probably the first person ever to sail out of the Mediterranean Sea into the Atlantic Ocean beyond. On the Atlantic coast of what is now Morocco, Hanno established seven Phoenician colonies. Many scholars believe that he also sailed along the Atlantic coast of Africa as far south as modern Sierra Leone.

HAWAII. Cluster of islands in the central portion of the Pacific Ocean, settled by Polynesian voyagers before A.D. 750. In 1778 Captain James Cook of England discovered the islands and named them the Sandwich Islands, in honor of the Earl of Sandwich. Cook and his men were the first Europeans to visit the islands.

HEARNE, SAMUEL (1745–1792). British fur trader who explored northern Canada. Hearne opened up unknown portions of Canada to settlement after leading a two-year expedition (from 1770 to 1772) to the mouth of the Coppermine River in the Mackenzie district of northwestern Canada.

HEDIN, SVEN ANDERS (1865–1952). Swedish explorer who wrote a number of scientific and popular works on his travels in Tibet, Sinkiang, and the Kunlun and Himalayan mountain ranges.

HENRY THE NAVIGATOR, PRINCE (1394–1460). Son of King John I of Portugal and a great patron of exploration. In 1416 Prince Henry established the Portuguese naval academies for the study of astronomy, geography, and navigation. He also encouraged Portuguese adventurers to explore the west coast of Africa and later Senegal and the Sudan. Prince Henry's chief contributions to history were his patronage and encouragement of world exploration and the development of the science of navigation.

HERJOLFSSON, BJARNI (10th century A.D.). Norwegian Viking trader. Herjolfsson was sailing from Iceland to Greenland in 986 when he was blown off course to the west. He reached a level country covered with woods that was probably somewhere along the Canadian coast. Herjolfsson returned to Greenland with tales of this fertile new land. His stories inspired other young men—including Leif Ericsson—to try to rediscover the place. Fifteen years later, in 1001, Herjolfsson sold his ship to Ericsson, who was planning to make the voyage along with some of the sailors who had accompanied Herjolfsson on the earlier trip.

HEYERDAHL, THOR (b. 1914). Norwegian adventurer. Although trained as an anthropologist, Heyerdahl became famous attempting to prove his theory that the first settlers of Polynesia came from South America. In 1947 Heyerdahl and five companions successfully sailed a primitive balsa-wood raft, called the *Kon Tiki*, from Peru to the Tuamotu Islands in the South Pacific, thereby demonstrating that the migration could have occurred as ancient Peruvian legends had described it.

In 1970 Heyerdahl and his companions again set sail—this time in a reed boat—from Morocco to the island of Barbados. This successful voyage proved that mariners in ancient times could have sailed from North Africa or the Mediterranean to the Americas, bringing their civilizations with them.

Heyerdahl has written several lively accounts of his adventures and explorations, including the books *Kon Tiki, American Indians in the Pacific, Aku-Aku, Sea Routes to Polynesia,* and *The Ra Expeditions.*

HILLARY, SIR EDMUND PERCIVAL (b. 1919). Mountain climber and explorer from New Zealand. In 1953 Hillary and Tenzing Norkay of Nepal became the first people to climb to the top of Mount Everest, the world's highest mountain peak (29,141 feet, or 8,742 m). In 1958 Hillary, with Sir Vivian Fuchs, led the first group to reach the South Pole by a land route since 1912. In 1960 he undertook an unsuccessful search in the Himalayas for the legendary Abominable Snowman.

HIPPALUS (c. A.D. 100). Ancient Greek merchant who observed the pattern of the monsoon winds in the Indian Ocean. Hippalus discovered that between May and October the winds blow steadily from the southwest, and that between November and March they blow from the northeast. This information was of immeasurable importance to early mariners sailing in the Indian Ocean between the Orient and ports on the Red Sea.

HUDSON BAY. Huge inland sea in east central Canada. The bay was discovered and explored in 1610 by Henry Hudson, who was looking for the Northwest Passage to the Orient. Later explorations by Pierre Radisson and his brother-in-law, Sieur de Groseilliers, from 1668 to 1670 led to the formation of the British Hudson's Bay Company to promote trade and settlement of the region.

HUDSON, HENRY (d. 1611). English navigator. In 1607 and again in 1608 Hudson was employed by the English Muscovy Company to try to find the Northeast Passage to the Orient. He was unsuccessful. Then in 1609 the Dutch East India Company hired him for the same purpose. He sailed his ship, the *Half Moon*, as far as Spitsbergen but because of the ice and cold could go no farther On his own, Hudson diverted his course to the west, crossed the Atlantic, and became the first European to sail up the great river later named for him. He traveled almost as far north as Albany and claimed the area for the Dutch. This led to the lively Dutch fur trade on the Hudson River and eventual settlement of the area by the Dutch.

In 1610 Hudson again sailed under an English flag and found Hudson Bay. While exploring the huge body of water in 1611, however, his crew, hungry and sick, mutinied and set him, his son, and seven loyal sailors adrift in a small boat. They were never seen again. Nevertheless, Hudson's explorations became the basis for England's claim to the Hudson Bay region of Canada.

Henry Hudson, d. 1611

HUMBOLDT, ALEXANDER, FREIHERR VON (1769–1859). German explorer and naturalist whose work initiated an era of systematic scientific exploration. Humboldt, trained as a scientist, kept careful records of all his observations. From 1799 to 1804 he led an extensive expedition to Cuba and Central and South America and conducted important early studies of these places.

HUNT, WILSON PRICE (1782?–1842). American explorer who led an overland expedition to Astoria, Oregon, from 1811 to 1812. Hunt was interested in finding a fast overland route between Astoria, the western fur capital, and St. Louis, Missouri, the center of the American fur trade. He discovered the Snake River Valley, which runs through southern Idaho and Oregon and toward the Pacific. This became the western part of the Oregon Trail, which many trappers and settlers followed into the American Northwest.

HYDROGRAPHY. The science of studying and charting large bodies of water such as oceans, seas, and rivers. Hydrographers survey, describe, and make maps that show currents, tides, coastlines, reefs, and other features of the ocean floor and shoreline. All of these factors are of keen interest to navigators.

IBN BATTUTA (1304?–?1378). Muslim traveler of the Middle Ages. No other traveler of the time is thought to have covered more territory than he did. Battuta is considered by some to have been the Islamic Marco Polo.

Beginning in his birthplace of Tangiers in modern Morocco, Battuta's travels took him across North Africa and through Syria and the Levant en route to the pilgrimage capital of Mecca in Arabia. He explored Arabia, Mesopotamia, Persia, and Asia Minor. He traveled to India by way of Samarkand and then on to China. Public honors were heaped upon him. He visited Sumatra and Ceylon, the Malabar coast, and the Maldive Islands.

Around 1350 Battuta returned to Tangier but later visited Spain, crossed the Sahara Desert, and traveled into Africa as far as Timbuktu and the Niger River. He marveled at the order, wealth, and power of the Mali Empire there and recorded all his observations in a lengthy dictated account called the *Rihlah*. This narrative, discovered many years later by the French, contains remarkably accurate information on the geography and customs of the lands he visited.

ICELAND. Large island in the North Atlantic between Greenland and the British Isles. Iceland may have been the *Ultima Thule* visited by the ancient Greek mariner Pytheas. Irish monks visited the island before A.D. 800, but Viking settlers claimed the land around A.D. 850.

JANSZOON, WILLEM (active 1600s). Dutch explorer who, along with other Dutchmen, sailed from Java and discovered Australia in 1605 or 1606.

JOLIET (or JOLLIET), LOUIS (1645–1700). New World explorer. Joliet was born in Quebec province but traveled to France as a young man to study the science of hydrography for a year. He returned to New France and became a trader and fur trapper in the Great Lakes region.

In 1673 Joliet led an expedition to search for the Mississippi, the mighty river the Indians spoke of. Joliet, Père Marquette, and five others set out for the regions of modern-day Michigan and Wisconsin, explored the Wisconsin River, then found the Mississippi and followed it south as far as the Arkansas River. They theorized that the Mississippi emptied into the Gulf of Mexico. They then crossed the river and followed its eastern bank as far as the Illinois River, tracing that river north to the area of present-day Chicago and finally returning to Lake Michigan.

Marquette stayed behind while Joliet traveled back East to report on the party's findings. Near Montreal Joliet's canoe overturned, and his journals of the expedition were lost. Joliet later wrote a brief narrative of the trip from memory, but the principal account of the exploration of the Mississippi was the one written by Marquette.

L

LAING, ALEXANDER GORDON (1793–1826). British army officer who in 1826 became the first European to cross the Sahara Desert and visit the west central African city of Timbuktu on the Niger River.

The trip was filled with perilous adventures. While crossing the Sahara, Laing's caravan was attacked, and Laing was the sole survivor. Badly wounded, he continued the journey alone, riding more than 400 miles (640 km) on his camel. He reached Timbuktu but never returned from it, since he was murdered near there, possibly by the native caravan leader who was to guide him back to North Africa. Nothing more is known of Laing's travels, since his journals and personal effects were never recovered.

LANDER, RICHARD LEMON (1804–1834). British explorer.

Lander began his career as personal valet to Hugh Clapperton during the latter's expedition to Nigeria. Clapperton died suddenly in 1827, but Lander made his way back to the coast from the central jungle after many hair-raising adventures. On one occasion a Yoruba chief forced Lander to prove his innocence by drinking poison. Fortunately, Lander vomited up the poison before it could kill him.

On his return to England in 1828, Lander published Clapperton's notes on the expedition along with his own account. He received the backing of the

British government to continue his explorations in Nigeria. From 1830 to 1831 he and his younger brother John explored central Nigeria and charted the course of the Niger River to its mouth on the Gulf of Guinea. For his discoveries Lander received the first medal ever bestowed by the Royal Geographical Society.

LA SALLE, ROBERT CAVELIER SIEUR DE (1643–1687). French explorer in North America. La Salle explored the Ohio Valley in 1669 and claimed it for France. In 1673 he was made commander of Fort Frontenac on Lake Ontario. He expanded trade and increased the number of French settlements. In 1682 he explored the entire length of the Mississippi to its mouth in the Gulf of Mexico and claimed the river and its valley for France. On a later expedition, in 1687, La Salle was murdered by his own men as he attempted to reach the mouth of the Mississippi from the Gulf of Mexico.

LEICHHARDT, FRIEDRICH WILHELM LUDWIG (1813–1848). Prussian-born German explorer who led the first successful overland expedition from southern to northern Australia. Leichhardt's party left Brisbane, on Australia's east coast, in 1844 and arrived at Port Essington, on the middle of the northern coast, fourteen months later. The expedition had covered nearly 3,000 miles (4,800 km) along a route that roughly follows Australia's northeastern coastline. In 1848, trying to cross central Australia from east to west, Leichhardt disappeared and was never seen again.

LE MAIRE, JAKOB (1585–1616). Dutch navigator who found a better way of rounding the southern tip of South America. Magellan had been the first explorer to sail around South America, but the Strait of Magellan that he used for his passage was a difficult route. Farther to the south Le Maire found a short and narrow seaway between Tierra del Fuego and the island of Staten Landt to the east. This passage is now called Le Maire Strait. Farther south is the open water of the Drake Passage, sighted in 1578 by Sir Francis Drake. Le Maire became the first person to navigate through the Le Maire Strait beyond Staten Landt and then southwest through the Drake Passage before heading up the western coast of South America. This became the established route for ships sailing to the Pacific until the Panama Canal was opened in 1914.

LEVANT. Old term for the Middle East, which comes from the Italian word for east, or the direction of the sunrise. The Levant was the area on the eastern shore of the Mediterranean Sea stretching from Egypt through Palestine, Lebanon, Syria, and Turkey.

**Meriwether Lewis,
1774–1809**

LEWIS, MERIWETHER (1774–1809). American explorer who was one of the leaders of the Lewis and Clark expedition. In 1801 President Thomas Jefferson appointed Lewis his secretary and in 1803 asked him to undertake an expedition across North America. Lewis asked his friend William Clark to help him lead the expedition, which left St. Louis in 1804. *See also* LEWIS AND CLARK EXPEDITION.

LEWIS AND CLARK EXPEDITION. Famous expedition in the early 1800s across the North American continent.

President Thomas Jefferson first conceived of the expedition. He wanted the territory he had just acquired from France, the Louisiana Purchase, to be explored, hoped to find a land route to the Pacific Ocean, and also wanted information gathered on the Far West and the Indian tribes who lived there.

Jefferson appointed his secretary, Meriwether Lewis, to lead the expedition. Lewis asked his friend, William Clark, to accompany him. The party set out from St. Louis in the spring of 1804, traveling up the Missouri River. An Indian woman named Sacajawea served as guide. The group reached the West Coast in the autumn of 1805 and spent the winter there preparing for the return journey. On the way back Lewis and Clark split briefly to follow separately the paths of the Marias and Yellowstone rivers. On September 23, 1806, they arrived back in St. Louis. Both Lewis and Clark kept careful records of their explorations, which added greatly to our early knowledge of the West.

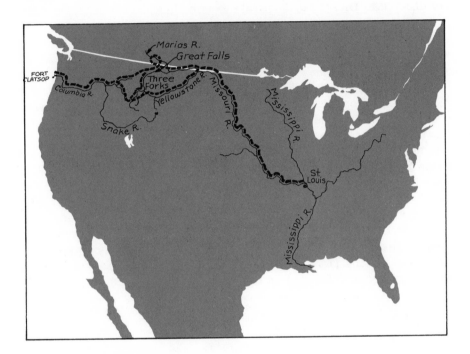

LINE OF DEMARCATION (PAPAL). To settle the disputes between King Ferdinand of Spain and King John II of Portugal over territorial claims, Pope Alexander VI in 1493 issued a bull, or decree, that divided up the non-Christian world between Spain and Portugal. The geography of most of the world was unknown at this time. The pope established a line of demarcation that extended from the North Pole to the South Pole one hundred leagues west of the Cape Verde Islands off the coast of Africa in the Atlantic Ocean. Spain had a right to any lands found west of this line, and Portugal could claim any lands to the east of it. In effect, Spain was granted the entire New World, and Portugal was entitled to all of Africa, India, and the Orient.

In 1494, however, the Treaty of Tordesillas, sanctioned by Pope Julius II, shifted the line of demarcation to a point 370 leagues west of the Cape Verde Islands. This enabled Portugal to assert a claim to Brazil—the eastern tip of South America—six years later, after the voyage of Pedro Cabral.

LIVINGSTONE, DAVID (1813–1873). Scottish physician and missionary and probably the best-known explorer of Africa.

Between 1840 and 1873 Livingstone preached and explored in Africa and made several important discoveries, writing about them in his book *Missionary Travels and Researches*. For example, he crossed the Kalahari Desert and found Lake Ngami in 1849. He discovered the Zambezi River in 1851, and in 1853 traveled along it, crossing the continent to Luanda on Africa's west coast. Crossing back, he discovered Victoria Falls in 1855 and continued on to Quilimane, Mozambique, on the east coast in 1856.

In 1859 Livingstone became the first Britisher to describe Lakes Chilwa and Nyasa in Malawi. On his final expedition, he returned to East Africa in 1866 to find the source of the Nile. He explored Lakes Nyasa and Tanganyika and was the first European to see Lakes Mweru and Bangweulu, in the area that is now Zambia. In 1869 Henry Morton Stanley was sent by an American newspaper to search for Livingstone after more than two years had passed with no news from him. He found him in November 1871, and the two went on together to further explorations. Livingstone died two years later, in Zambia, and his body was brought back to England for burial in Westminster Abbey.

MAGELLAN, FERDINAND (c. 1480–1521). Portuguese navigator who became an explorer for Spain. Magellan was captain of the first ship to circumnavigate the globe. Magellan himself did not live to complete the voyage, but one of his ships, the *Victoria*, and a greatly reduced crew did return to the Spanish port of their departure after a harrowing voyage that lasted for three years.

**Ferdinand Magellan,
c. 1480–1521**

On September 20, 1519, Magellan sailed from Sanlúcar de Barrameda with five ships and about 270 men. He reached the coast of South America and in January 1520 explored the mouth of the Rio de la Plata, to rule out the possibility that it might be a shortcut to the Pacific Ocean. In October 1520 he found the Strait of Magellan.

Magellan died in the Philippines in 1521, killed by feuding natives. Juan Sebastián del Cano, captain of the *Victoria*, assumed leadership of the expedition and completed the voyage, arriving in Spain in September 1522.

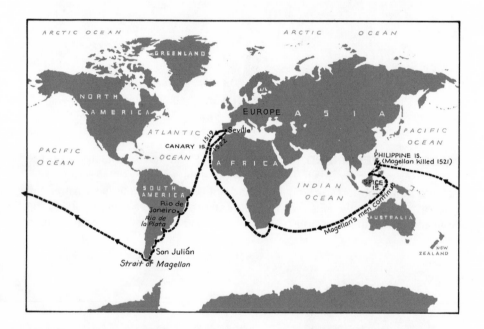

MAGNETIC POLES. Either of the two polar areas of the northern and southern hemispheres toward which the needle on a compass always points if you are anywhere near that magnetic pole. The magnetic poles do not correspond exactly to the geographic poles of the earth's axis.

MANDEVILLE, SIR JOHN (d. 1372). Fourteenth-century English author of one of the most popular books of the Middle Ages, *The Travels of Sir John Man-*

deville. Mandeville completed his great travelog around 1356. He wrote it in Norman French, the language introduced into England by William the Conqueror and his knights. Soon the book was translated into the English of that time (Middle English), Latin, and many other European tongues.

Mandeville's work tells colorful stories of travels through the Holy Land, Egypt, India, China, and of a sojourn in the African court of a Christian monarch he called Prester John. The book is full of strange legends, fictitious people, and misinformation.

Scholars now think Mandeville never made any of the journeys he wrote about but relied heavily upon the accounts of other travelers, including Marco Polo, to piece together his account.

MARQUETTE, JACQUES (also called PÈRE MARQUETTE) (1637–1675). French Jesuit priest who first came to North America as a missionary in 1666. Marquette studied several Indian languages before setting out in 1668 from the Trois Rivières settlement in New France (eastern Canada) to minister to the Ottawa Indians of the Great Lakes region. He stayed at La Pointe for more

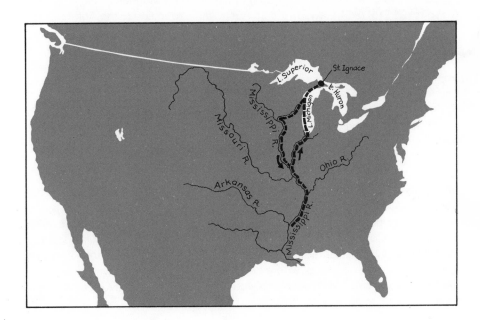

than two years before moving on to found a new mission at Point St. Ignace in Mackinac in 1671.

In 1673, Louis Frontenac, the governor of New France, appointed Marquette to accompany Louis Joliet on an expedition to trace to its mouth the great south-flowing river—the Mississippi—the Indians often spoke of. In May 1673 the two men and their party set out and soon found a water route that took them all the way from the St. Lawrence River across the Great Lakes to the Wisconsin River and from there to the mighty Mississippi River. They reached the mouth of the Arkansas River 700 miles (1,120 km) upriver from the mouth of the Mississippi on the Gulf of Mexico and returned to Lake Michigan in September 1673 by way of the Illinois River.

MAWSON, SIR DOUGLAS (1882–1958). Australian geologist and Antarctic explorer who was born in England. In 1903 Mawson made his first geographical expedition, to the New Hebrides. From 1907 to 1909 he was a member of Sir Ernest Shackleton's expedition to Antarctica and was one of the party that scaled Mount Erebus, Antarctica's great volcanic mountain peak. He also accompanied Shackleton on his quest for the South Magnetic Pole.

From 1911 to 1914 Mawson led an Australian expedition to the Antarctic. He was one of an exploratory party of three that discovered King George Land. Mawson survived the grueling expedition, but his two assistants perished.

From 1929 to 1930 Mawson commanded a joint expedition of scientists from Britain, Australia, and New Zealand. On this expedition he explored Enderby Land, an area that had not been visited for a century, and discovered the MacRobertson Coast. Using a seaplane, he surveyed over 1,000 miles (1,600 km) of uncharted coast and remapped large sections of coastline that had only been roughly known before. Mawson's explorations are the basis for Australia's claim to a large portion of Antarctica.

MENDAÑA DE NEYRA, ALVARO DE (1541–1595). Spanish mariner who sailed from Peru in 1567 in an attempt to repeat a legendary voyage undertaken by the tenth-century Inca ruler of Peru, Tupac Yupanqui. Mendaña de Neyra discovered the Solomon Islands in the southwest Pacific and returned to Peru. On a voyage some twenty-five years later, he discovered first the Marquesas Islands and then the Santa Cruz island group, where he tried to establish a colony. However, he died, the colony failed, and the islands were forgotten for nearly two centuries until Philip Carteret rediscovered them in 1767.

NANSEN, FRIDTJOF (1861–1930). Norwegian naturalist and explorer.

In 1888 Nansen and a party of five became the first Europeans to cross Greenland on skis. Nansen wanted to reach the North Pole, and in 1893 he tried his startlingly original plan of drifting north in the ice across the polar basin in a ship, the *Fram*, specially designed to resist being crushed by ice. This plan was not successful, so he tried to complete the journey by sled. He reached a latitude of 86° 14′ before being turned back by icy conditions. This was, however, the northernmost point to have been reached at that time.

Nansen achieved worldwide fame for his explorations and added much to our scientific understanding of the Arctic region. More importantly, he proved that the North Pole is surrounded by a frozen sea, the Arctic Ocean. He also laid the foundations for future Arctic exploration with his meticulous studies of Arctic weather and oceanography and his development of survival strategies, including suggestions for the kinds of clothing and diet best suited to prolonged work in the far north.

NEW ALBION. During his circumnavigation of the globe, Sir Francis Drake landed on the coast of California in 1579 in the general area of San Francisco Bay. Not knowing that the Spanish had asserted a previous claim to the area, he named the region New Albion, after Albion, a poetic name for England. English navigational charts continued to identify California as New Albion well into the eighteenth and nineteenth centuries.

NEW FRANCE. In general, the name given to the parts of Canada—especially the St. Lawrence Valley and Quebec—discovered, explored, claimed, and colonized by the French, beginning with Jacques Cartier in the mid-1530s.

NEW FRONTIERS IN EXPLORATION. Modern explorers face the challenge of exploring the universe and possibly finding unknown civilizations on the planets of distant suns. But there is still a huge frontier on the face of the earth—the virtually untouched world beneath the sea. And there remain some land areas on the surface of the globe that have still not been completely explored or charted. These are remote places, where the climate or geography make travel difficult even for hardy adventurers. Polar explorations are still underway. Eastern Tibet may contain mountain peaks even higher than Mount Everest—the Amne Machin in the Himalayas may be one such mountain. Portions of Africa's interior as well as the islands of Dutch New Guinea are little known. Even the highly developed Philippine Islands have yielded startling discoveries of previously unknown cultures in recent years. And in the New World, the tropical rain forests of South America and portions of the Andes, Ecuador, Peru, Paraguay, Colombia, Venezuela, and the Guyanas await further investigation. The explorers of tomorrow will have to face some of humankind's greatest challenges.

NEW WORLD. Term for the Western Hemisphere, particularly the landmasses of North and South America, first heavily explored by Europeans in the Age of Discovery—the fifteenth to the eighteenth centuries.

NICOLET, JEAN (1598?–1642). French explorer who came to New France (eastern Canada) with Samuel de Champlain in 1618. In 1634 Nicolet became the first European to pass through the Straits of Mackinac—the passage between the upper and lower peninsulas that form the modern state of Michigan and that connects Lake Michigan with Lake Huron. Nicolet explored Lake Michigan; its inlet, Green Bay; and the Fox River. He drowned at Trois Rivières, a major French trading post set up where the St. Lawrence and St. Maurice rivers flow together in southern Quebec province.

NILE RIVER. World's longest river, over 4,000 miles (6,400 km) in length. Two branch rivers, the White Nile and the Blue Nile, flow together at Khartoum in the Sudan to form the Nile River. The valley of the river Nile—the ancient land of Egypt—was a cradle of civilization. But the sources of the Nile remained a mystery for centuries. The ancients believed that the river flowed from the mysterious "Mountains of the Moon" in east central Africa.

It was not until the eighteenth and nineteenth centuries that explorers thoroughly charted the Nile's course and found its sources in Africa's interior. In 1770 James Bruce, the Scottish explorer, identified the source of the Blue Nile at Lake Tana, in Ethiopia. The British explorer John Speke discovered and explored the sources of the White Nile at Lake Victoria and Ripon Falls in east central Africa during three separate expeditions—in 1854, from 1857 to 1859, and again in 1962.

NORDENSKJÖLD, NILS ADOLF ERIK (BARON) (1832–1901). Swedish explorer.

Nordenskjöld was born in Finland of Swedish parents. As a young man he studied geology and accompanied several expeditions to Spitsbergen, a group of islands in the Arctic Ocean.

After 1864 Nordenskjöld led a number of expeditions to the polar regions. He prepared maps of Spitsbergen and gathered an extensive collection of Arctic animal, plant, and mineral specimens and fossils. He also explored portions of Greenland's interior, and in the course of his journeys he traveled farther north than anyone had previously done.

In 1872 Nordenskjöld began a search for a Northeast Passage to serve as a trade route to the Pacific. On a series of voyages he crossed the Kara Sea and explored the Yenisei River. In 1878 he sailed as far as the Bering Strait before being stopped by ice. In 1879 he sailed through the strait and completed the voyage to China. In recognition of his accomplishments, the Swedish king made him a baron in 1880.

On later expeditions Nordenskjöld explored the ice barrier off Greenland's east coast and traveled once again to Spitsbergen. During the last twenty years of his life, he wrote a number of interesting works on travel and exploration.

NORKAY, TENZING (b. 1914). Nepalese mountain climber who served as guide on Sir Edmund Hillary's expedition to the summit of Mount Everest, the world's highest mountain. In 1953 he and Hillary became the first people ever to reach the top.

NORTH AMERICA. In prehistoric times, perhaps as far back as 50,000 years ago, people of Asiatic origin came to inhabit the Americas by crossing over into Alaska from northeastern Asia. European exploration and settlement in North America date back to the Vikings, who colonized Greenland in A.D. 986 and visited the eastern coast of Canada around A.D. 1000.

Columbus first sighted land in the New World in 1492, probably the land that is today Watlings Island in the Bahamas, southeast of Florida. He later explored portions of the West Indies and Central America. John Cabot explored eastern Canada in 1497. This was probably the first recorded European landing on the North American continent after Columbus' time.

Numerous Spanish and French expeditions followed. In 1513 Juan Ponce de Leon discovered Florida and explored much of it, searching for the Fountain of Youth. In 1524 Giovanni da Verrazano sailed along the midsection of the American east coast between Florida and Maine. Jacques Cartier made three voyages for France, starting in 1534, and explored the St. Lawrence regions of Canada that would later become the colony of New France. From 1520 to 1521, Hernán Cortés, in addition to his conquest of the Aztec empire, made the first comprehensive exploration of Mexico. Around 1540 two Spanish explorers in North America, Francisco de Coronado and Hernando De Soto, explored the southwestern and southeastern portions of what is now the United States. Garcia López de Cárdeñas discovered the Grand Canyon.

In the early years of the seventeenth century, Henry Hudson explored the area that is now eastern New York State and discovered Hudson Bay in northern Canada. From 1605 to 1608 Samuel de Champlain explored much of the Atlantic coast of Canada, and New England as far south as Martha's Vineyard. On various expeditions later in the seventeenth century, Louis Joliet, Père Marquette, and Robert La Salle explored the Mississippi River.

In the eighteenth century Sieur de la Vérendrye investigated central Canada. George Vancouver, Robert Gray, and Alexander Mackenzie explored large portions of northwestern North America.

After the United States purchased the Louisiana territory from France in 1803, the Lewis and Clark expedition explored much of western North America, areas that would eventually become states. Later explorers concentrated on smaller sections of the American frontier and made many valuable discoveries exploring mountains, lakes, rivers, and trade routes.

NORTHEAST PASSAGE. Water route, connecting the Atlantic and Pacific oceans, that extends from the North Sea in Europe, along the Arctic coast of Asia, and through the Bering Sea to the Pacific. The Northeast Passage was sought by many early European explorers as a shortcut to the Orient. Sir Hugh Willoughby and Willem Barents in the sixteenth century, Henry Hudson in the seventeenth century, and Vitus Bering in the eighteenth century all tried unsuccessfully to find the passage.

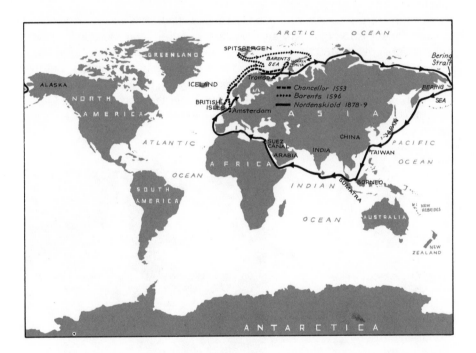

Baron Nils Adolf Erik Nordenskjöld of Sweden made the first successful passage through the channel, in 1878–1879, sailing east along the northernmost coast of Russia and through the Bering Strait. Clogged with ice for most of the year, the passage is navigable only from June through September, unless icebreaker ships are used. The Russians mapped, explored, and made the Northeast Passage into a regular shipping route. It is still used somewhat by the shipping industry but has lost much of its former importance with the development of air commerce.

NORTH POLE (ARCTIC REGIONS). Northernmost tip of the earth's axis. The North Pole is not a landform but a frozen section of the ocean.

The search for the Northeast and Northwest passages led a number of explorers into the Arctic regions in the sixteenth century. Ice-clogged waters defined the upper limits of their voyages. The Northeast Passage was finally found during a voyage undertaken by the Swede Nils Nordenskjöld from 1878 to 1879. The Northwest Passage was first negotiated by the Norwegian, Roald Amundsen, from 1903 to 1906.

Later explorers sought to reach the North Pole itself. This was accomplished by Commander Robert Edwin Peary on April 6, 1909, after more than eleven years of attempts. In 1831 Sir John Ross fixed the location of the North Magnetic Pole on the Boothia Peninsula in the Arctic regions of Canada, but this was more than 1,000 miles (1,600 km) from the North Pole. In 1926 the American pilot, Richard E. Byrd, made the first flight over the North Pole. On March 17, 1959, the U.S. nuclear submarine *Skate* surfaced through the ice at the North Pole.

Richard E. Byrd (1888–1957) was the first person to fly over the North Pole. In the photo he is shown dressed in his white admiral's uniform.

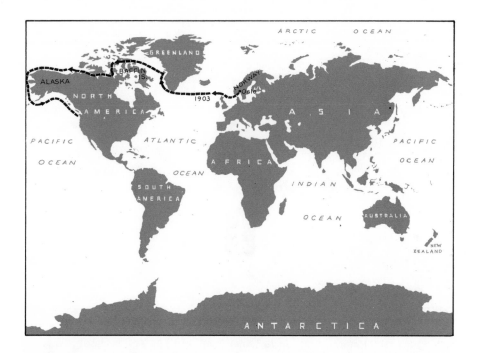

NORTHWEST PASSAGE. A North American sea route to the Orient sought by European mariners, who wished to sail directly from the Atlantic Ocean to the Pacific Ocean without having to go around the southern tip of South America. The search for the Northwest Passage prompted many navigators to undertake voyages of exploration in the sixteenth and seventeenth centuries, including Sir Martin Frobisher and Henry Hudson. Sir John Franklin of England came within a few miles of the passage on an expedition from 1845 to 1848 and is sometimes credited with being its discoverer. However, the Norwegian, Roald Amundsen, was the first to successfully go through the passage, in a voyage lasting from 1903 to 1906.

OJEDA, ALONSO DE (1465?–1515). Spanish adventurer and explorer who sailed on Columbus' second voyage to the New World. On an expedition with Amerigo Vespucci and Juan da la Cosa from 1499 to 1500, Ojeda explored the northeastern coast of South America as far west as the Gulf of Venezuela. In 1505 he explored the Gulf of Darien off the eastern coast of Panama. Ojeda was later responsible for establishing several Spanish settlements in Central America.

OREGON TRAIL. The 2,000-mile-long (3,200-km) overland route from the Missouri River westward to the Columbia River. It was this route that was followed by American pioneers as they moved westward to settle the section of territory known as Oregon Country, a region claimed by both Britain and the United States. Fur trappers were the first to use this route, but it assumed importance only after farmers and others became interested in settling Oregon Country.

Wagon trains of settlers set out from various points in Missouri, including Independence, Kansas City, Westport, and St. Joseph. Mountainmen—fur trappers and traders in the Rockies—developed the route in the 1820s and 1830s. Jim Bridger and others served as guides who led settlers in the 1840s through the dangerous mountain passes and difficult river crossings that characterized the Oregon Trail. The trail fell into disuse in the 1870s, after railroad service was extended to the Northwest.

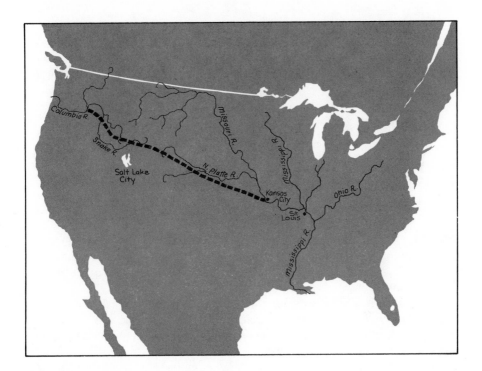

ORELLANA, FRANCISCO DE (d. ?1546). Spanish conquistador who aided in the conquest of Peru. In 1538 Orellana helped lead an expedition into South America's interior. He and his party separated from the main expedition when they arrived at the Napo River, a tributary of the Amazon, in 1540. Orellana and his detachment sailed down the big river and arrived at the Amazon's mouth on the Atlantic coast in 1541. Rumors of tribes of female warriors prompted the Spanish to name the river Amazon, after the warlike women of Greek mythology. A few years later, probably in 1546, Orellana was attacked and killed by hostile Indians as he attempted to return up the river.

PACIFIC OCEAN. The world's largest ocean, extending from the north to the south polar areas and from the western coasts of the Americas to the eastern shores of Asia and Australia. The Pacific covers nearly one third of the surface of the earth.

The vast Pacific Ocean was first sighted in 1513 by Vasco Nuñez de Balboa, after he and his men had marched across the Isthmus of Panama. He claimed the "Great South Sea" and all the lands washed by its waters for Spain. Seven years later Magellan renamed the huge body of water the Pacific, meaning "peaceful" or "calm." Today the term South Sea(s) refers only to the southern portion of the Pacific.

In 1565 Andrés de Urdaneta discovered the winds that blow steadily across the Pacific in certain latitudes and that can serve as a key to navigating the great ocean. Mendaña de Neyra crossed and recrossed the Pacific, from Peru to the Philippine Islands, in two expeditions in the sixteenth century and discovered the Solomon, Marquesas, and Santa Cruz island groups. Pedro de Quirós found the New Hebrides in 1606. Sir Francis Drake, Abel Tasman, William Dampier, James Cook, Vitus Bering, and George Vancouver discovered the major islands of the Pacific and roughly defined the outline of the ocean by the end of the eighteenth century. Captain James Cook was perhaps the most distinguished explorer of the eighteenth century. On several prolonged voyages in the Pacific he sighted Antarctica, explored the coasts of New Zealand and eastern Australia, and discovered the Hawaiian Islands.

PARRY, SIR WILLIAM EDWARD (1790–1855). English navigator and second in command to Sir John Ross on the 1818 British naval expedition in search of the Northwest Passage to the Orient. The following year Parry commanded his own expedition and became the first explorer to force his way through the icy, choked waters of Lancaster Sound to Melville Island, the main geographical discovery of his career. Solid ice stopped him 300 miles (480 km) short of completing his journey to the Pacific.

In his several expeditions into the far north, Parry made many useful discoveries. He was the first to note the westward drift of the Arctic ice pack; the first to propose the use of dogsleds and ships mounted on runners for Arctic exploration; and he came within 500 miles (800 km) of the North Pole, one of the closest distances attained in the nineteenth century.

PEARY, ROBERT EDWIN (1856–1920). American explorer of the Arctic.

Peary first became interested in polar exploration when he visited Greenland in 1886 as a civil engineer for the U.S. Navy. From 1891 to 1892, while on leave from the Navy, Peary commanded an expedition to Greenland and made important scientific observations regarding the weather and the Eskimos living there.

Peary made a lengthy expedition from 1893 to 1895 and two shorter trips in 1896 and 1897. These explorations yielded further scientific discoveries concerning Greenland and the polar regions.

Peary gained support for expeditions into the Arctic to study the polar ice pack from 1898 to 1902 and 1905 to 1906 and drew progressively nearer to the North Pole, his ultimate goal. On April 6, 1909, he succeeded in reaching the North Pole; with him were one servant and four Eskimo guides. Congress recognized Peary's claim as first person to reach the North Pole, although Dr. Frederick A. Cook, who had accompanied Peary on an earlier expedition, claimed to have reached the pole in April 1908.

PHOENICIANS. An ancient Mediterranean people who originally lived in cities along the coast of what is now Syria. Many historians think the Phoenicians were the first true explorers.

By 1100 B.C. Phoenician ships were sailing all around the Mediterranean and Red seas, mostly in an effort to increase trade. The Phoenicians were the first known mariners to pass through the Strait of Gibraltar into the Atlantic Ocean. Phoenician sailors ventured far north in Europe, visiting the British Isles, where they traded for tin from the mines of Cornwall. They established settlements wherever they found a market for their goods, and Phoenician colonies sprang up in Sicily and Sardinia as well as along the coast of Africa. Carthage was the most important city in North Africa. The Phoenicians also settled in Cadiz, on the coast of Spain.

Around 600 B.C. Phoenician ships may have sailed from the coast of the Red Sea in Egypt all around Africa from east to west. In the fifth century B.C. they sailed down the west coast of Africa as far south as the Gulf of Guinea, establishing many settlements along the way. But the Phoenicians kept their discoveries a secret to prevent rivals and pirates from threatening their monopoly on trade with the new areas they had found.

PIKE, ZEBULON MONTGOMERY (1779–1813). American Army officer and explorer. From 1806 to 1807 Pike led an expedition through the Southwest into Colorado and discovered Pike's Peak. Because it rises from the edge of the Great Plains, Pike's Peak is the most conspicuous mountain peak in the Rockies, although not the highest.

PINZÓN, MARTÍN ALONSO (1440?–1493). Spanish navigator who commanded the *Pinta* on Columbus' historic voyage to the New World. His younger brother, Francisco Martín, also sailed on the *Pinta* and served as ship's master. Shortly after returning to Spain, Martín Alonso Pinzón died.

PINZÓN, VICENTE YÁÑEZ (1460?–?1524). Spanish navigator who commanded the *Niña* on Columbus' first voyage to the New World. Columbus continued on board the *Niña* after the *Santa Maria* was wrecked. Pinzón was the brother of Martín Alonso Pinzón, who commanded the *Pinta* on the same trip.

In 1500 Vicente Pinzón returned to South America, where he discovered the mouth of the Amazon River. On an extended voyage from 1508 to 1509 he explored the coasts of Yucatan, Honduras, and Venezuela. He was accompanied on this voyage by another Spanish explorer, Juan Díaz de Solís.

PIZARRO, FRANCISCO (c. 1476–1541). One of the most famous of the Spanish conquistadors and the conqueror of Peru. On early expeditions to the New World, Pizarro accompanied Alonso de Ojeda to Colombia in 1510 and

Vasco Nuñez de Balboa on his march across Panama to the Pacific Ocean in 1513.

After exploring the coastal regions of Peru, Pizarro returned to Spain in 1528. There he told Charles V about the fabulous wealth of the Inca Empire in the Andes Mountains of South America. In 1531 he set out, with the sanction of Charles V, to conquer Peru and the Incas. He took his three brothers—Gonzalo, Juan, and Hernando—and a large force. They arrived in Peru in 1532 and soon became friendly with Atahualpa, the Inca emperor. But Pizarro later had Atahualpa executed for refusing to convert to Christianity.

In 1533 Pizarro and his men marched to Cuzco, captured the city, and carried away vast amounts of gold and treasure, including priceless art and religious objects, thus destroying one of the most advanced civilizations in the New World. In 1535 he founded Lima, the new capital of Peru. That same year he dispatched his lieutenant, Diego de Almagro, to conquer Chile. Pizarro had already mistreated Almagro several times, and when Almagro returned with no booty, Pizarro had him put to death. Soldiers loyal to Almagro plotted against Pizarro and assassinated him in 1541.

Francisco Pizarro, c. 1476–1541

POLO, MARCO (1254–1324). Famous Italian traveler of the thirteenth century from the city-state of Venice.

Marco Polo's father Niccolo and his uncle Maffeo, both merchants, first journeyed to the Orient in 1266, after a war prevented them from returning to Venice from a trade expedition to Constantinople. They were received in China by the Mongol chief, Kublai Khan, at his capital, Kaifeng. Three years later they returned to Venice with wonderful tales of Oriental splendor. In 1271 they launched another expedition to the Khan's court, this time accompanied by the young Marco Polo and two Roman Catholic priests. At this time, the Khan's huge empire encompassed India, China, and most of Asia.

In 1275 the Polos reached the Chinese city of Cambuluc (modern Beijing). The Khan took a liking to young Marco and used him to conduct business in various parts of his empire. Marco was appointed ruler of the city of Yangchow for three years. After a twenty-year absence, the travelers returned to Venice in 1295.

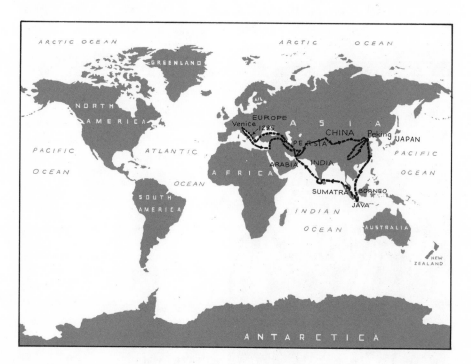

During a Venetian war against Genoa in 1296, Marco Polo was taken prisoner. He was held captive for two years, but he used this time to compose and dictate a book about his travels. The book describes parts of the world virtually unknown in Europe at the time, including the Middle East, Persia (now Iran), Japan, Sumatra, the Andaman Islands, and, of course, China. Polo also traveled through many parts of eastern Africa and as far south as Zanzibar during his long absence from Venice. He vividly described the customs of the peoples he had observed and many products as yet unheard of in Europe, including gunpowder, coal, paper, paper money, and asbestos.

During the Renaissance, Polo's book was the West's main source of information about China and the Orient. Many parts of Asia visited by Marco Polo remained unexplored by other European travelers until the late nineteenth century.

PONCE DE LÉON, JUAN (c. 1460–1521). Discoverer of Florida.

Ponce de Léon was the Spanish governor of Puerto Rico between 1509 and 1512. Legends of a magical "Fountain of Youth" prompted him to secure permission from the Spanish crown to explore the island of Bimini. Since no map existed pinpointing Bimini, Ponce de Léon sailed from Puerto Rico in 1513 and reached the coast of the North American mainland near the modern city of St. Augustine. He named the area *La Florida*, since the discovery was made during Easter week. (In Spanish, Easter is often called *Pascua Florida,* or "Feast of Flowers." He then returned to Puerto Rico, again missing the island of Bimini, which is some 40 miles (64 km) off the southeastern coast of Florida.)

In 1521 Ponce de Léon sailed to Florida with two shiploads of settlers. Unfortunately, the party was attacked by hostile Indians. Many of the settlers were killed, and Ponce de Léon was mortally wounded. The group fled to Cuba, where Ponce de Léon died a short time later.

PYTHEAS (or PYTHIAS) (4th century B.C.). Greek explorer and geographer who sailed northward around the coast of Europe and discovered Britain in 330 B.C. Pytheas sailed beyond Iceland about 100 miles (160 km) into the Arctic Circle. In an account of his voyages, he described the coasts of the Netherlands and the British Isles. He is credited not only with the discovery of Britain but also with helping to prepare what were probably the world's first accurate maps and navigational charts.

Q

QUIRÓS, PEDRO DE (1565–1615). Portuguese by birth, de Quirós first served in 1595 as the Spaniard Mendaña de Neyra's chief pilot and later led his own expedition for Spain in search of a mysterious continent said to lie in the South Pacific. In 1605 he discovered the Tuamotu Archipelago in the south central Pacific and in 1606 the New Hebrides Islands near the eastern coast of Australia. It was more than a century and a half until the New Hebrides were visited again, by Louis Bougainville in 1768.

RADISSON, PIERRE ESPRIT (1636?–1710). French explorer of North America. Radisson was kidnapped by Indians when he was a teenage boy living in the French settlement of Trois Rivières in Quebec province. For several years he lived among the Indians and learned the ways of the forests. After returning to the French settlement in 1651, he became a fur trapper and trader. He and his brother-in-law Groseilliers explored various sections of the Midwest. They discovered the source of the Mississippi and were the first Europeans to set foot in the areas that are now northern Nebraska and the Dakotas.

After the French governor cheated Radisson out of a fortune in furs in 1660, Radisson defected to England but returned to the Hudson Bay region on a later expedition. His glowing reports of the potential riches in furs and other wealth inspired many others to seek their fortunes in the New World, and his accounts encouraged the English to form the Hudson's Bay Company and to assert their claims in Canada.

RICHTHOFEN, BARON FERDINAND VON (1833–1905). German geologist, geographer, and explorer who surveyed the length and breadth of China during a period when the Chinese were particularly hostile to foreigners. Between 1868 and 1872 Richthofen made seven trips through China and then spent seven years compiling the first complete modern atlas of the country.

ROGGEVEEN, JACOB (1659–1729). Dutch explorer who searched for a great continent that Europeans theorized lay in the South Pacific between South America and Australia. On Easter Sunday, 1722, he discovered Easter Island, 1,000 miles (1,600 km) from the west coast of South America. The island is covered with huge, mysterious stone statues erected many centuries ago by the Polynesians. For half a century Easter Island was ignored. Then Don Felipe González, a Spanish naval captain, rediscovered it in 1770.

ROHLFS, FRIEDRICH GERHARD (1831–1896). German adventurer and explorer who was the first European to penetrate into many parts of Africa and the Sahara.

In Arab disguise Rohlfs reached Tafillelt, Morocco, and Tidikelt in the Tuat oases of southern Algeria. In the years 1865 to 1867 he became the first European to cross the African continent by land and reach the Gulf of Guinea. In the 1870s he led two important German expeditions to Egypt and Libya. Rohlfs' explorations opened up new portions of Africa to European contact and trade and corrected many geographic misconceptions about the locations of certain ancient African cities.

ROSS, SIR JAMES CLARK (1800–1862). English explorer active in Antarctica. Ross was a nephew of the explorer Sir John Ross, accompanied his uncle on many voyages, and made five polar expeditions before he was thirty years old. In 1831 he located the North Magnetic Pole in Canada's Boothia Peninsula.

From 1839 to 1843 Ross commanded a British expedition to the South Magnetic Pole, spending nearly five years investigating Antarctica and its waters. He discovered Ross Island and the Ross Sea, named for him, as well as Mount Erebus and the region of Antarctica named Victoria Land. Erebus was named after one of his ships. Ross penetrated farther south than any previous Antarctic explorer had done and compiled important data about the earth's magnetic field.

ROSS, SIR JOHN (1777–1856). British rear admiral and Arctic explorer who discovered the Boothia Peninsula, the Gulf of Boothia, and King William Island during a voyage from 1829 to 1833 in search of a Northwest Passage to the Pacific. In 1831, with his nephew Sir James Clark Ross, he established the location of the North Magnetic Pole on the Boothia Peninsula.

S

SAAVEDRA, ÁLVARO DE (d. 1529). The first New World explorer to sail from America to the Orient. Saavedra crossed from Mexico to the Philippine Islands in 1527.

On the return trip in 1529 he discovered the Marshall Islands but then fell ill and died. His crew turned back before his ship had located the westerly winds that would have carried them eastward across the Pacific. It wasn't until nearly forty years later that another Spanish explorer, Andrés de Urdaneta, would discover the best route eastward across the Pacific.

SACAJAWEA (active 1804–1806). The Indian woman who served as guide on the Lewis and Clark expedition. Her name is generally thought to mean ''Bird Woman'' in English.

As guide on the expedition, Sacajawea often kept the party from becoming lost and helped them through many difficult situations. With her knowledge of the terrain and superior survival skills, she was particularly helpful during the crossing of the Rocky Mountains. And when a canoe carrying the party's records capsized, it was Sacajawea who saved many of the journals and instruments that had fallen into the water. She thus preserved an important record of the trip.

SCHOMBURGK, SIR ROBERT HERMANN (1804–1865). British explorer who was born in Germany. A trained naturalist, Schomburgk led an expedition to British Guiana (now the Republic of Guyana) in 1835 to collect botanical and geographical information about the colony. From 1841 to 1843 he conducted a survey of the colony and established the boundaries of the country, although they were later disputed by neighboring Venezuela.

SCHOUTEN, WILLEM CORNELIS (1567?–1625). Dutch navigator who left Holland with Jakob Le Maire in 1615 to search for an alternate route to the Pacific Ocean. At that time the Dutch East India Company held a monopoly on trade with the Indies.

Le Maire and Schouten sailed beyond the Strait of Magellan and around the southern tip of South America, which they named Cape Horn, after Hoorn in the Netherlands, Schouten's birthplace. Crossing the Pacific, Schouten explored the northern coasts of New Ireland and New Guinea and other islands nearby. He had discovered a new route, but the East India Company claimed that their rights had been violated. Later Schouten's ship was seized in Java, and Schouten himself was arrested.

SCHWEINFURTH, GEORG AUGUST (1836–1925). German explorer who from 1869 to 1871 traveled through various parts of the Congo and Sudan in central Africa and discovered the Uele River. Schweinfurth was the first European to cross between the basins of the Nile and Congo rivers.

Schweinfurth rediscovered the African pygmies, who had been mentioned by the Greek writer Herodotus in the fifth century B.C. but had not been seen by Europeans for over 2,400 years. He also stumbled upon groups of cannibals. Although he lost his scientific instruments during the return trip from this expedition, he was still able to measure the distance he had traveled—by counting his footsteps, more than 1,250,000 of them!

SCOTT, ROBERT FALCON (1868–1912). Officer in the British Navy who commanded an expedition from 1901 to 1904 to explore the Ross Sea region of Antarctica. In 1910 he set out again, this time determined to reach the South Pole. He and four companions succeeded in reaching it on January 18, 1912, only one month after Roald Amundsen. On the return journey Scott and his party perished in a blizzard, only 3 miles (4.8 km) from their base camp. The remains of the men and their records of the journey were later recovered.

SEVEN CITIES OF CIBOLA. Legendary Indian cities of great wealth in the New World.

Francisco de Coronado was governor of one of the Mexican provinces when he heard reports from Fray Marcos de Niza, a Franciscan friar, of Indian cities of fabulous wealth located to the north. These stories excited Coronado's interest, and in 1540 he led an expedition to search for the treasures of the Seven Cities of Cibola. Fray de Niza served as a guide in the search.

Coronado fell into disgrace when the expedition proved fruitless. All that the Spaniards found in looking for the fictitious cities were the humble villages of the Pueblo Indians in the Southwest and another Indian village (Quivira) in what is now Kansas. Old legends of the Zuni Indian tribes were the origin of the stories of the fabled Seven Cities of Cibola.

SHACKLETON, SIR ERNEST HENRY (1874–1922). British explorer of Antarctica.

Shackleton accompanied Robert Scott on his Antarctic expedition from 1901 to 1904. From 1907 to 1909 he commanded his own expedition to the South Pole regions and used sturdy Manchurian ponies in place of dogsleds in his attempt to reach the South pole. But the last of his ponies fell into a deep crevasse only 97 miles (155 km) short of his goal, and Shackleton had to abandon his dream of being the first to reach the Pole. Still, he had accomplished more than any earlier explorer had done. In addition, members of his party pinpointed the South Magnetic Pole and scaled the 13,370-foot-high (4,011-m) volcano, Mount Erebus.

From 1914 to 1917 Shackleton planned to cross the whole of the Antarctic continent, from the Weddell Sea to the Ross Sea by way of the South Pole, but this expedition was marked by disaster from start to finish. World War I broke out just before the expedition was about to be launched, and Winston Churchill, then First Lord of the British Admiralty, had to order Shackleton not to abandon the project. Shackleton's vessel was crushed by ice and sank shortly after the party arrived at the Weddell Sea. Shackleton showed incredible heroism in leading five of his men in a 22-foot (6.6-m) open rowboat over 800 miles (1,280 km) of icy seas to safety at the whaling station on South Georgia Island. A little over four months later he returned to rescue the rest of the group. From 1921 to 1922 Shackleton commanded an expedition to Enderby Land but died of a heart attack near the coast of South Georgia Island in the South Atlantic.

SHEPARD, ALAN BARTLETT, JR. (b. 1923). American astronaut. Shepard was a graduate of the U.S. Naval Academy and a naval officer when he was selected to be an astronaut for the U.S. space agency, NASA, in 1959. Shepard became the first American to be launched into space—on a suborbital mission on May 5, 1961. He flew inside the Mercury *Freedom 7* capsule in a mission that lasted fifteen minutes.

SOLÍS, JUAN DÍAZ DE (d. 1516). Spanish navigator who in 1514 was commissioned to find a passage from the Atlantic to the Pacific coasts of South America. In 1516 he discovered the mouth of the Rio de la Plata on the southeastern coast of South America. After sailing into the river's estuary, he and a small party landed on the coast of what is now Uruguay, and Solís was killed by hostile Indians.

SOUTH AMERICA. Continental landmass in the Western Hemisphere chiefly south of the equator.

It is not certain who was the first European to reach South America. Columbus explored portions of the northern coast on his third voyage to the New World. And Amerigo Vespucci may have explored parts of the South American coast in 1499 or 1501. Pedro Cabral discovered Brazil in 1500 and claimed it for Portugal. But Vicente Pinzón, earlier that same year, had also reached Brazil, and he explored the mouth of the Amazon River. Early in 1516 Juan de Solís discovered the Rio de la Plata, between Argentina and Uruguay. Francisco Pizarro explored and conquered the Andean empire of the Incas between 1531 and 1535. In 1535 Diego de Almagro landed on the coast of Chile, and Pedro de Valdivia led an expedition into the country itself in 1540. Francisco de Orellana became the first explorer to penetrate the interior of South America, investigate the length of the Amazon River, and cross South America from west to east.

In the last quarter of the sixteenth century, Antonio de Berrio, in search of the legendary wealth of El Dorado, explored much of Colombia and Venezuela. Between 1799 and 1804, Alexander Humboldt, the great German naturalist, investigated many areas of Central and South America, and from 1841 to 1843 Robert Schomburgk surveyed Guyana and claimed it for Great Britain.

SOUTH POLE. Southern tip of the earth's axis.

The South Pole is in roughly the middle of Antarctica. It was first reached on December 14, 1911, by Captain Roald Amundsen of Norway, traveling by dog-sled and on skis. Admiral Richard E. Byrd made the first airplane flight over the South Pole, in 1929. *See also* ANTARCTICA.

SPACE EXPLORATION. On October 4, 1957, the Soviet Union launched the earth's first artificial satellite, *Sputnik I*, beginning the space age. The United States launched its first satellite, *Explorer I*, on January 31, 1958. Up until this time telescopes had collected all the information we had about the stars, planets, moons, and other celestial bodies of the universe. Scientists today are exploring space with numerous kinds of artificial satellites, space probes, and spacecraft, all launched into space by powerful rockets.

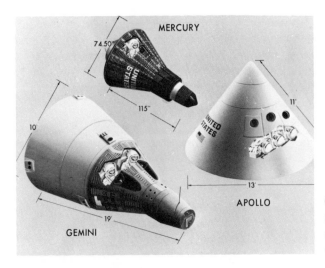

Comparative sizes and shapes of the *Mercury*, *Apollo*, and *Gemini* spacecraft

In recent years space probes equipped with cameras and other instruments have landed on the moon, Venus, and Mars and have had flyby encounters with Mercury, Jupiter, and Saturn. The U.S. Mariner program did important early studies of Venus and Mars in the 1960s. Exploration of Mars continued in the 1970s with the Viking program for unmanned spacecraft that landed on the surface of the planet. Automated labs inside the *Viking* landers conducted extensive experiments there. In the early 1980s the Russians successfully landed several *Venera* spacecraft on the surface of Venus.

The era of manned space exploration began with the orbital flight of the Soviet cosmonaut Yuri Gagarin on board *Vostok 1*, on April 12, 1961. The U.S. Mercury program began in 1960 with suborbital missions. In February 1962 John Glenn circled the earth three times. In May 1963 a U.S. space flight lasting for twenty-two orbits was completed. In 1965 the first space missions involving more than one astronaut were attempted by both the American and Soviet space programs. The first active docking of two spacecraft in space was accomplished in 1966.

The Apollo space program was undertaken in 1961, when President John F. Kennedy committed the United States to a goal of landing a man on the moon by the end of the decade. The *Apollo 11* spacecraft was launched on July 16, 1969, from the National Aeronautics and Space Administration (NASA) center at Cape Kennedy (now Canaveral) in Florida. Four days later, on July 20, 1969, Neil Armstrong and Edwin Aldrin became the first humans to walk on the surface of the moon, as the command module *Columbia*, manned by a third astronaut, Michael Collins, remained in orbit around the moon. The *Apollo 11* mission and later *Apollo* flights all returned safely to earth with samples of lunar rock and a large amount of scientific information.

Edward H. White II, on a *Gemini* flight, became the first American to "spacewalk."

An active program of manned space exploration was resumed in 1977 with the Space Shuttle, designed to carry people, supplies, and equipment into orbit around the earth and back home again. A U.S. space station will eventually be built to remain in orbit while the reusable Shuttles ferry astronauts and scientists back and forth from space. By the end of 1982, four successful return journeys had been made.

In the early 1980s the two unmanned U.S. *Voyager* spacecraft made flyby encounters with the planets Jupiter and Saturn and many of their moons, sending back spectacular photographs of the gas giants. One of the *Voyagers*, it is hoped, will rendezvous with Uranus in 1986.

Space exploration is only in its infancy. The moon is the only place outside the earth that people have actually visited, but there is the whole solar system, with its asteroids and moons, and perhaps even other planets similar to our own in other solar systems, waiting to be explored.

SPEKE, JOHN HANNING (1827–1864). English explorer in Africa. In 1858, accompanied by the adventurer Sir Richard Burton, Speke discovered Lake Tanganyika. Later that same year, he discovered the huge lake, Victoria Nyanza, in east central Africa. Lake Victoria is one of the chief sources of the river Nile.

SPITSBERGEN. Cluster of islands in the Arctic Ocean, some 400 miles (640 km) north of the Norwegian mainland. Spitsbergen was discovered by the Vikings in the twelfth century but was largely forgotten until Willem Barents rediscovered the islands in 1596. Henry Hudson passed through them in 1607 while looking for the Northeast Passage to the Orient.

STANLEY, SIR HENRY MORTON (1841–1904). British-born American journalist and explorer who had come to the United States as a boy of fifteen.

In 1869 Stanley was working for the *New York Herald* when the owner of the newspaper, James Gordon Bennett, commissioned him to go to central Africa to search for David Livingstone, the Scottish missionary and explorer who had not been heard from for more than two years. In November 1871 Stanley found Livingstone in a village near Lake Tanganyika and greeted him with the now-famous words: "Dr. Livingstone, I presume?" He and Livingstone explored Lake Tanganyika until 1872, when Stanley returned to the United States.

In 1873 Stanley was commissioned by Leopold II of Belgium to continue explorations in Africa. He returned to Africa in 1874, and in 1875 he explored

Lake Victoria Nyanza and Lake Tanganyika and then followed the Lualaba and Congo rivers to the Atlantic coast. He was the first European to trace the Congo to its mouth, setting up trading stations in the area. He made two more expeditions to Africa, from 1879 to 1884 and again from 1887 to 1889, and in 1889 he discovered the Ruwenzori range, the so-called "Mountains of the Moon" in east central Africa.

Stanley finds Livingstone and greets him with the famous words, "Dr. Livingstone, I presume?"

STEIN, MARK AUREL (1862–1943). Hungarian-born archaeologist and geographer who became a British subject. In a series of expeditions between 1900 and 1930 he explored and excavated sites along the Silk Route, the unused overland route between the West and China. One of his discoveries was the ancient temple complex called the Cave of the Thousand Buddhas, where he found priceless early religious texts and other treasures. Stein explored many unknown parts of Sinkiang, northeastern Tibet, and the western Kansu region of China.

T

TASMAN, ABEL JANSZOON (1603?–1659). Dutch navigator. Between 1632 and 1653, Tasman made many voyages to places in the Pacific and Indian oceans for the Dutch East India Company, carrying on trade and exploring new lands. On a voyage that lasted from 1639 to 1642 he sailed around the coast of Japan, visited Taiwan and the Philippine Islands, and discovered a number of small islands.

In 1642 Tasman sailed with two ships from the Dutch port at Batavia in Java and discovered New Zealand and another large island he called Van Diemen's Land. Van Diemen's Land is now called Tasmania, in the explorer's honor. During this same voyage he made a stop at the Tonga Islands and sailed around Australia. Until this time many people believed that Australia was part of a continent that extended all the way to the South Pole. Tasman returned to Batavia in 1643. The following year the Dutch East India Company sent him on another voyage to gather more information about the geography of Australia and its position in relation to New Guinea and Tasmania. Tasman's findings helped others to chart the southwestern Pacific Ocean.

THORFINN KARLSEFNI (active A.D. 1002–1015). Icelandic Viking leader who tried to colonize North America.

Karlsefni went to Greenland in 1002 and married Gudrid, the widowed daughter-in-law of Eric the Red. Around 1010 he set out with three ships and a hundred and sixty men to search for and settle Vinland, the fertile country that had been discovered by Leif Ericsson a few years earlier. Two Icelandic sagas tell of Karlsefni's exploits.

According to the sagas, Karlsefni first arrived at a region called Helluland, which means "flat stoneland" in Old Norse. Next he came to Markland, a forested country. South of Markland he found areas of sandy beaches that he called Furdustrands. For two years Karlsefni's Viking party traveled southward, looking for Vinland, the land of grapes. After battles against the native Indian tribes in which two of the Vikings were killed, Karlsefni and his party returned northward to the bay they called Straumfjord. From there they returned to Greenland via Markland.

There is much controversy as to the actual places Karlsefni visited. Their probable locations are somewhere between Labrador and New England.

TORRES, LUIS VAEZ DE. Spanish navigator of the seventeenth century. Torres sailed from Peru in 1605 and discovered the Torres Strait, the passage in the Pacific between the island of New Guinea and the northern coast of Australia. In 1774 Captain James Cook rediscovered the strait.

TUPAC YUPANQUI (active A.D. 1000?). Inca ruler and conqueror who sailed across the Pacific Ocean from Peru on a balsa-wood raft and returned with a fortune. He lived centuries before Columbus and became the subject of a lively Inca legend. The tales of his exploits inspired Alvaro de Mendaña de Neyra of Spain to seek his fortune in the South Pacific in the sixteenth century.

In 1947 Thor Heyerdahl repeated the voyage of the fabled Inca on a balsa-wood raft called the *Kon Tiki*, purported to be a replica of the craft used by Tupac Yupanqui.

ULLOA, FRANCISCO DE (active 1539). Spanish explorer.

Sent by Hernán Cortés in 1539, Ulloa sailed from Acapulco on the Pacific coast of Mexico into the Gulf of California. He discovered the mouth of the Colorado River and sailed around the Gulf of California and about 700 miles (1,120 km) up the coast of Baja (Lower) California. Ulloa made the first successful exploration of the southwest coast of North America. His voyage showed that Baja California was a peninsula belonging to the North American continent and not a separate island.

UNDERSEA EXPLORATION. Underwater exploration began in ancient times. Aristotle wrote of divers who descended 100 feet (30 m) to retrieve sponges. In 1819 the diving suit and helmet were invented so that divers equipped with air tubes could plunge to new depths. Underwater construction workers, salvagers, and pearl fishers welcomed these inventions. The British *Challenger* expedition of 1872 to 1876 marked the beginning of the modern science of oceanography.

Study of the ocean bottom and of marine life forms is now possible because of the development of specialized vessels and equipment. The era of manned exploration of great ocean depths began in the 1930s, when William Beebe and Otis Barton descended to a depth of 3,000 feet (900 m) in a bathysphere.

A bathysphere is a round, watertight observation chamber made of steel and equipped with windows. It can be lowered to the bottom of the sea, enabling divers to observe the plants and animal life there. An undersea expedition in 1952 discovered a canyon at the bottom of the Atlantic Ocean comparable in size to the Mississippi River.

The *Glomar Challenger* (above), a modern research ship, was designed to increase our knowledge of the geology of the eastern Atlantic sea floor. The *Alvin* (right) is a small navy research submarine that can dive deep to explore the ocean bottom.

In the 1940s the Swiss scientist Auguste Piccard developed the bathy-scaphe. This is a deep-sea diving apparatus equipped with a steel observation chamber that can descend without a cable to great depths. A lead-weighted balloonlike chamber filled with a fluid lighter than water—usually gasoline—is used to raise and lower the bathyscaphe. In 1960 a bathyscaphe descended 35,800 feet (10,740 m) to the Challenger Deep of the Marianas Trench in the western Pacific Ocean.

Modern aqualungs, or scuba equipment, developed after World War II by the great French oceanographic explorer Jacques Cousteau and now greatly improved, enables divers to descend safely to points on the ocean floor 600 feet (180 m) below the surface.

The most recent underwater research vessels are similar to small subma-rines. They can carry crews of two to six people, cameras, and scientific equipment and can investigate the ocean floor at depths of up to 8,000 feet (2,400 m). Naval oceanographic research teams have established temporary stations on the ocean bottom, to test the ability of humans to withstand under-water life.

Knowledge of the ocean is important to shipping, fishing, defense, and communications. Naval and commercial oceanographic programs drill cylindri-cal core samples from the ocean floor and analyze them for mineral content. Undersea exploration has enabled scientists to chart large areas of the ocean floor, preparing contour maps that show that it is even more varied than dry land. In addition, scientists have found there many strange and exotic forms of sea life as well as important deposits of oil and valuable minerals.

URDANETA, ANDRÉS DE (1508–1568). Spanish navigator. On his first Pacific crossing, Urdaneta was one of a party of Spanish traders who traveled through the Strait of Magellan westward across the Pacific to Indonesia in 1525, making use of the trade winds that blow constantly from east to west in the tropical latitudes. Not knowing how to return, they found themselves stranded in Indonesia until 1536.

Some thirty years later, in 1565, Urdaneta navigated a Spanish fleet from Mexico to the Philippine Islands. He returned by sailing north to Japan and there discovered the prevailing westerly winds that blow eastward in the North Temperate Zone. He was able to return swiftly to the coast of California, thus establishing a route followed by all vessels crossing the Pacific until the intro-duction of steam travel in the nineteenth century.

VANCOUVER, GEORGE (1757–1798). English navigator and explorer. From 1791 to 1794 Vancouver commanded an expedition into the Canadian northwest to take over the Nootka Sound territory seized by the Spanish in 1789. Vancouver explored and surveyed large areas of northwestern Canada and opened up the northern Pacific coast to British settlement. A city in Canada was later named for him.

VERRAZANO, GIOVANNI DA (c. 1480–c. 1527). Italian navigator from Florence employed by the French in 1524 to look for a Northwest Passage to Asia. Unsuccessful in his attempt, he did explore the Atlantic coast of North America between Nova Scotia and North Carolina and was probably the first European to sail into New York Bay through the Verrazano Narrows, now spanned by one of the world's great suspension bridges.

In 1526, again sailing on behalf of the French, Verrazano explored the West Indies, where he was attacked by natives and killed. Information gained from his discoveries, however, helped his brother Gerolamo, a cartographer, to prepare a more accurate map of North America in 1529.

VESPUCCI, AMERIGO (1454–1512). Italian-born explorer. Under Spanish patronage Vespucci made a voyage to the New World in 1499. He sailed alongside Alonso de Ojeda but separated from him shortly before they reached the West Indies.

Continuing south, Vespucci discovered and explored the mouth of the Amazon River. He then investigated the northern coast of South America as well as many Caribbean islands. On a voyage undertaken in 1501, he explored the southern coast of South America for Portugal.

In 1507 the German cartographer Martin Waldseemüller first used the name America on a map of the New World. This was in honor of Vespucci's discovery that South America was a separate continent and not just a part of Asia.

Vespucci was a brilliant navigator who developed a new system for computing longitude. He also estimated the earth's circumference with remarkable accuracy.

VIKINGS. Around A.D. 800, several groups of Scandinavians called the Vikings, Northmen, or Norsemen, began a flurry of exploration to find adventure plus new homelands for a fast-growing population that their own land could no longer support. They were expert seamen and set out in long, graceful, narrow, open boats called *knarrs* that could either be sailed or rowed.

The Vikings became great colonizers in the Middle Ages. They crossed the Baltic Sea into Russia and sailed up and down that country's rivers. Crossing the North Sea, they settled in France in the province of Normandy and in the British Isles, where they were regarded as the marauding Danes. They even sailed as far south as the Mediterranean and founded trading colonies in Sicily. They ventured farther out into the Atlantic than earlier sailors had dared to go.

Around 850 the Vikings colonized Iceland. Around 982 Eric the Red, a Viking leader exiled from Iceland, discovered Greenland and colonized its west coast. Using Greenland as a base, Viking mariners sailed farther west and reached the shores of North America around 986 and again in 1001 and explored an area they called Vinland, or Wineland, which has yet to be accurately identified. Bjarni Herjolfsson, Leif Ericsson, and Thorfinn Karlsefni were among the most important Viking explorers in America.

VINLAND. North American land briefly colonized by the Vikings.

There is overwhelming evidence that around A.D. 1000 Leif Ericsson visited the eastern coast of North America and found a land where grapes and wheat were growing. Later Thorfinn Karlsefni tried to rediscover the same land.

Places ranging from Newfoundland to Virginia have all been suggested as possible locales for Vinland. Although no one is certain just where it is, it is generally thought today to have been somewhere along the southern coast of New England. A stone tower in Newport, Rhode Island, might be the remains of a Viking settlement, but it might also date from a later period.

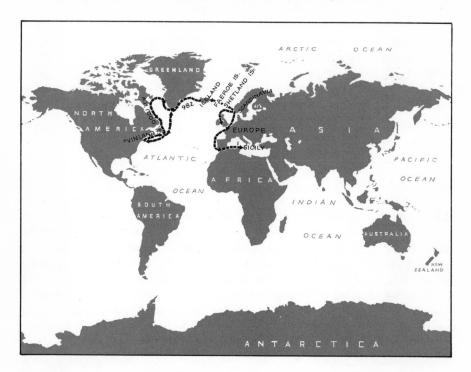

WALKER, JOSEPH REDDEFORD (1798–1876). Tennessee-born fur trader, trapper, and explorer of the Far West. Walker was the discoverer, in 1833, of California's Yosemite Valley, famous for its giant sequoia trees. He also discovered a pass through the mountains of the Sierra Nevada that is called Walker Pass in his honor.

In 1843 Walker led one of the first wagon trains into California through the pass he had found. This route later became part of the usual trail settlers followed through the Sierra Nevada and into California's Central Valley.

WALLIS, SAMUEL (1728–1795). English explorer who crossed the Pacific in search of a new continent in 1766. Wallis explored the Tuamotu Archipelago and discovered several new islands in the group, including Tahiti. His route across the Pacific took him more than 1,000 miles (1,600 km) southwest of any previous voyage undertaken by a European.

WEDDELL, JAMES (1787–1834). British navigator and seal hunter who in 1823 discovered the Weddell Sea, an arm of the Atlantic Ocean southeast of South America and bordered by the easterly portion of the Antarctic ice shelf.

YERMAK (or ERMAK) TIMOFEEV (d. 1584). Leader of an independent band of eight hundred Russian Cossacks. Like himself they were all soldiers of fortune, and many of them were violent criminals fleeing from justice. Yermak began his career as a river pirate on the Volga.

In 1581 Maxim Stroganov, the head of a wealthy Russian merchant family, obtained a royal patent to seize Siberia from the Mongols. Siberia was the center of a lively trade in furs and walrus ivory. The Stroganovs chose the fearless Yermak and his Cossacks to lead the expedition.

In 1582 Yermak and his band, armed with guns, crossed the Urals and captured Sibir, the capital of the Tartar Khanate. Yermak was killed in an outbreak of fighting between the Tartars and the Cossacks in 1584. But he had already explored much of western Siberia, and, under the protection of Czar Ivan IV, Siberia was opened up to settlement by Cossacks and other Russian groups.

YOUNGHUSBAND, SIR FRANCIS EDWARD (1863–1942). British explorer in central Asia. In 1887 Younghusband traveled extensively from China to India, over the Gobi Desert, and later in Mongolia and Tibet. In 1904, on a military expedition to Tibet, he persuaded the Dalai Lama to sign a treaty with Great Britain that opened the country to Western trade.